# CLUELESS TO COMMISSIONED

A Female Officer's Journey with God through
Fifteen Years with the Fort Worth Police
Department

Kelly A. Martin

authorHOUSE®

*AuthorHouse™*
*1663 Liberty Drive, Suite 200*
*Bloomington, IN 47403*
*www.authorhouse.com*
*Phone: 1-800-839-8640*

*First published by AuthorHouse 1/2/2009*

*ISBN: 978-1-4389-2956-9 (sc)*

*Printed in the United States of America*
*Bloomington, Indiana*

*This book is printed on acid-free paper.*

# Contents

# Dedications

**For my family:** my husband, Steve Martin; my mother, Edith Horn; my mother and father-in-law, Suzie and Coy Martin; my sister and brother-in-law, Carla and Don Strawn; my nieces, Allison and Jennifer; my "adopted" sister, Karen Kline and her husband Troy; my "adopted" nieces, Hannah and Courtney; my granny, Dorothy Craig; my aunt Shirley and uncle Donald McGowan; my aunt Doris; my aunt Frances, aka "Auntie Fixit;" I also wish to acknowledge my many cousins and other extended family – especially Darla Brown and Kenneth Justice who have put service to God high on their list of priorities;

**For my church family at Beach Street Baptist Church:** Including Pastor Nathaniel Daves; The Seekers' Class (who are like real brothers and sisters); Cherrie Call, who feeds us from both God's Word and from her own kitchen every Sunday morning; Louise Delaney and Maddy White, (two angels I have actually met in person); Maggie Baggs, my "Mrs. America;" and every other member of my loving church family;

**For my friends and colleagues from all walks of life:** Some of you have lifted me from the bottomless pit of my own ignorance by extending your loving arm to me in my darkest hours of need. Others of you have been priceless to me during the brightest and best times in life. Many of you have done both: John Douglas (J.D.) Angle; Alana Baxter, Nikki Belshe, The Birmingham Family; The Burch Family; Beth Call; Andy Cecrle; Brenda Charon; Michael Conley; Maria Conley; Donna Cottongame; Birta Deaton; Karen Duke; Jennifer Estill; Tom Fort;  Sheila Gonzales; Shelia Guckian; Marlen Gutierrez; Randy Harvison; Pam Harvison;  Roger Hawkins; Wanda Hawkins; Bettye Haynie; Trisha Jenkins; Eric Jewell; Andro Kemp; Kelley Kirby; Staci Koetter; Rick Lopez; Dee Lopez; Amy Marken; Mamie Marks; Edna McCloskey; Samantha Moran; Emily Moran; John O'Rourke; Kavita Panchal, David Peacock; Judy Peacock; Brenda Phillips; Adrian Previte; Laurie Ray; Travis Shelton; Annette Shully; Jackie Sims; Darla Smith; Sunnye Simmons; Gloria Vasquez; Gregg Vines; Gloria Vines; Jennifer Ward; Kim Wester; Chris Willars; Leticia Willars; Jill Willis; Celeste Wilson; Sylvia Wheat; Karen Winkler; Amy Womack; Carrie Wright; Pam Wylie; *A special group of ladies (you know why!):* Layne Falkenberg; Robin Bass; Jin-Ju Choi; Renee Edwards; Jennifer Murphy-Hall; Inakali Kiba; Jessica Harvey-Matz;

**For my fellow F.W.P.D. officers who have been an important part of my career and life:** J.R. Barron; David Bell; Bryan Bice; J.W. "Whit" Boyd; Didi

Broadus; Clay Buckelew; Ron Carey; Henry Castaneda; Scott Cryer; Wilson Daggs; Jerry Dalton; Rachel Dehoyos; Glenn Edney; Renee Evans-Jacoby; Ken Flynn; Cathy Fowler; Danny Garcia; Irene Garza; Larry Goodwin; Jon Grady; M. Harkrider; Jan and Mike Hiebert; Kathi Hopson; Darryl Horn; Bryan Jamison; Gary Jeandron; Brad Johnson; Judy Jones; Joe Loughman; Maricelia Maldonado; Gwen Maxwell; Dorcia Meador; Bob Redding; J. Pete Rost; C.C. Ryder; Maria Salinas; D.J. Scott; Michael Shunk; Sara Straten, Bob Sutherland; Margaret Terry; Lawrence Thomas; Kathy Thompson; David B. Walters; Tom Wiederhold; Jon White;

**For my mentors:** One may not realize when his or her actions become instrumental in transforming another person's life. You have provided me with both insight and example: My Mother and prayer warrior, Edith Horn; Jim Brown, Dr. Jon Crook; Frances Dawson; Dr. Scott Floyd; Charles Fowler; Brenda Fowler; John Harvison; Rance McCloskey; Lt. John O'Rourke; Sgt. S. Mark Smith; Bill Truesdale; Carolyn Truesdale; Dr. Shannon Wolf; All of my public school teachers in the City of Haltom City;

**For those who have gone to be with the Lord:** My father, Gilbert L. Horn; My pastor, Richard L. Call; Santina "Sandy" Barranco; George Bolden; Kimberly Hardin; Floyd Kirby; Evelyn Temple; Richard "Dick" Williams; *Fellow Fort Worth Police Officers*: Officer Alan Chick; Officer Dean Christensen; Officer Dana Downard; Officer Dwayne Freeto; Officer Sean Lee; Detective Donald Manning; Officer John Paul Marcellus, Officer J.D. Moorman; Officer Hank Nava; Detective Roger Spivey; Officer Brent Wisdom; Officer Paul J. Zoldak; and all other FWPD Officers who gave their lives and service to our City;

I dedicate the efforts and the message of this book to everyone who has been a part of my world. Without each one of you, none of the circumstances of my life would have fallen into place as God intended. I believe that everyone who touches our lives, even for merely a brief encounter, is a test of our witness to our Lord. God created each of you as a special masterpiece and for a special purpose in His kingdom. You are important to Him and He loves you. Likewise, you are important to me, and I love you. I thank you for being who you are, knowing that without you, this book would not be possible.

# Preface

Unfortunately, the art of storytelling is quickly fading into obscurity, becoming a phenomenon of the past. Hidden amongst the shadows of time is the once honored tradition of sitting around the dinner table discussing the events of the day with the family. Even more uncommon is the act of taking the time to sit around listening to cherished stories of life in the "good old days" with older generations of relatives. Time with grandparents is often lost to video games, the Internet, television, and even to sports, school work and other legitimate responsibilities. Parents struggle to make it through the work, school, athletics, and church week, in a seemingly never ending cycle. Quality time often falls prey to the sheer exhaustion that these responsibilities bring. Priorities have shifted, especially as technology has continually and exponentially advanced during our era. Distractions are rampant, and the simple pleasures of life have been shrouded by the grandeur of the next bigger television screen, the next smaller phone, and the more innovative, faster, and more functional electronic gadgets.

Despite the decline in appreciation for them, from very early history it has been clear that stories are important for the furtherance of human learning, in general. Jesus told stories to the multitudes gathered around to hear His teaching.

*"And they were astonished at his [Christ's] doctrine: for he taught them as one that had authority…"* (Mark 1:22)

He used stories to strategically illustrate points of wisdom and instruction. Writers of Scripture use inspired narratives to provide stories from biblical history that give us the ability to understand the roots of our faith.

One of the most enjoyable treats in my life comes on Saturday mornings. Once or twice each month, my husband, Steve and me hop eagerly into the truck with my father-in-law, Coy Martin, and begin the hour-or-so trip to Jack County. The highlight of the day is a stop at Herd's, a little burger shop in downtown Jacksboro. After eating a sinfully delicious grease-soaked burger, we move on down the dirt-roads of Jack County towards what is affectionately deemed, "the farm." Our arrival there brings a few responsibilities and many simple pleasures as we tend to the land and the surrounding wildlife.

My father-in-law served for well over thirty years in law-enforcement in the Fort Worth area, and Steve is still an officer after twenty-six years and counting. As a result, those road trips are often peppered with enthusiastically recounted "war stories" or sometimes just reminiscent thoughts of some of the more famous moments of the past. It is always a pleasure to relive the memories along with my father-in-law as he enthusiastically recounts those stories, always making a point to emphasize the same highlights - the ones which made the biggest impression on him. What a treat and a gift it is to listen to him travel back in time.

Too many people miss out on the value of the knowledge our older generations have cultivated throughout their lives. At the risk of sounding cliché, I must assert that we rarely appreciate the value of things around us until those things are gone. Through this assertion, I am referring to the knowledge, life-lessons, and memories of our ancestors. Even if this statement *is* cliché, how is it possible that its truth still does not elicit a change in the way we act, despite its obvious wisdom? Why do we still not make it a point to visit with our elders and have meaningful conversations with them more often?

I have no children with whom to share my life experiences (and I certainly don't have a lot of wisdom). However, I do have exciting memories and stories to tell, and a desire to share these stories with loved ones and others so that future generations will have a small glimpse of how things were in years past. As a result, this book showcases some of the more memorable incidents, calls, and predicaments I have experienced during my fifteen year career as a Fort Worth Police Officer.

Most would never have believed I would end up in this position, not in a million years. This was evidenced during my ten year reunion from Haltom High School when I was awarded the *"Most Surprising Career"* title after a vote by my former classmates.

During my high school years I was shy and bashful and made an art form out of blending in with the crowd and basically disappearing, altogether. As recently as my twenty year high school reunion there were those who surprisingly proclaimed, "I never knew you! Were you in our class?"

While I was indeed timid, quiet, and always compliant with rules and directives, I still couldn't hide from my sinful nature. I had selfish and misdirected desires, a lack of wisdom and responsibility, and an unfortunately low regard for the fact that I was a child of God.

I had a group of friends who were very responsible, smart and altruistic. Although that group was not perfect, my high school friends were some of the best people I have ever known. As a matter of fact, I still keep in touch, on some level, with most of them. We were never incorrigible by any stretch; however, the normal level of teen mischief was never underachieved.

While I am certain that the statute of limitations has passed, my recollection of one particular incident from our past still brings dread, guilt, and a sick feeling in the pit of my stomach. I write this with hesitation, but the confession will indeed be very good for my soul.

One night when my friends and I were out for a routine joyride, listening to music, and planning our next snack of junk food, we had an amazingly bright idea. As we passed by the home office of an extremely lucrative and prominent soft drink manufacturer in north Fort Worth, the shining brass letters that spelled out the name of this mega-enterprise were too inviting for us to ignore. The brightly illuminated display seemed to beckon us forth, with a magnetic force. As a result, the car stopped right in front of it.

Despite every lesson I had ever learned in my home, school and church, I exited the car, along with one of my other friends to commit a thrilling, yet meaningless theft. We approached the huge concrete block upon which the letters were prominently displayed, under the illumination of spotlights. I began to pull on the letter from one end, my friend pulled from the other. Very quickly we were able to loosen the screws that held that first letter onto the display. I often wish that letter had been more heartily secured. If it had taken us longer than ten seconds, we would have abandoned this shameful foolishness. Unfortunately, it was too easy, and we were almost immediately successful. Feeling a rush of excitement at our accomplishment, we carted the letter, which was made of solid brass-plated steel and measured about three feet long, and somehow crammed it into the trunk of my friend's car.

There were two other of my very good friends in the car, and they just sat in complete disbelief as we stole this very expensive ornament from the front of this business. Why did we do it? There was absolutely no reason. None of us could display the letter in our room. None of us would sell it. None of us could even remove it from the trunk of this car without getting the third degree from a guardian. So what ever became of that very expensive ornamental letter? It was thrown in a dumpster to avoid our being caught. What a waste. What ignorance. What guilt I still feel for having taken an integral part in that crime.

Even now, twenty-something years later, I still feel guilty and ashamed for taking part in such a disrespectful and meaningless act. It is clear to me that the convicting power of the Holy Spirit is ever omnipotent. Although my friend and I were never caught for this crime, my guilt has never faded. This truth only highlights the fact that when we sin against God, there *is no* statute of limitations. The guilt is there until we ask for forgiveness. Even then our wavering human nature sometimes makes it impossible to feel completely exonerated.

Even though very few people knew about the incident I just revealed, still hardly anyone who knew me in school would have ever pegged me as someone who would someday wear a badge. I didn't expect it, either. However, I am a Christian, and I do believe that my path has been (and is still being) directed. Even though it seemed completely out of place in my life, I am quite confident that my law enforcement career was planned for me. Actually, the passage of my life has led me trudging tentatively through many unexpected turns.

Over time, my crooked dirt path of uncertainty has become a winding road of adventure. Each stop along that road has brought growth, wisdom, and a little more understanding of how this world works. As I progress through these lessons of life, I am continually transformed. I have already changed from a naïve, overprotected child into a strong-willed woman who has survived a variety of complicated challenges. For a long time I did not realize that the knowledge I gained from these challenges might someday be useful for the benefit of others. I was able to cultivate reliance upon God to carry me through the tough assignments He often placed before me. Over time, my ability to trust Him has become more pronounced. Consequently, the more I trust Him, the more He uses me. The letter in Scripture, written by James, tells us, "*Whereas ye know not what shall be on the morrow. For what is your life? It is even a vapour, that appeareth for a little time, and then vanisheth away.*" (James 4:14)

I am thankful for the opportunity to grow closer to God as

He molds my short and "vaporous" existence here on this earth into something for His purposes and within His kingdom. The following passage describes perfectly how my life has been directed by the Lord's provision. This has been true for me even in times when I did not understand why my path led to a place where I had to take one of those uncertain forks in the road:

*When my spirit was overwhelmed within me, then thou knewest my path. In the way wherein I walked have they privily laid a snare for me. I looked on my right hand, and beheld, but there was no man that would know me: refuge failed me; no man cared for my soul. I cried unto thee, O LORD: I said, Thou art my refuge and my portion in the land of the living. Attend unto my cry; for I am brought very low: deliver me from my persecutors; for they are stronger than I. Bring my soul out of prison, that I may praise thy name; (Psalm 142:3-7)*

# Disclaimer

Some who will read this book are accomplished law enforcement officers who are accustomed to dealing with the concepts of undesirable language, drug use, violence and sexual activity on a daily basis. Others, however, will perhaps not be in a position to have dealt with such issues. As a result, things that might be considered second nature for many readers will be unexpected and offensive for others. Although I have made every effort to exclude as much questionable content as possible, sometimes (for the development of the context), the inclusion of this type of content is necessary. Out of respect for those who might wish to avoid such issues, I have placed warning tags at the beginning of segments that contain such material that *might be* considered questionable. I choose to warn readers because I want to observe the following caution and directive from scripture that says, *"Abstain from all appearance of evil." (1 Thessalonians 5:22)* I do not want anyone to stumble upon something which, in his or her opinion, may be inappropriate or that will be offensive.

Furthermore, the incidents provided herein depict the highest level of accuracy possible, although some accounts have been embellished slightly for storytelling purposes. Names have been changed for the anonymity of the officers, as well as the citizens involved. Even so, these events are being depicted much as they actually happened. Unfortunately, over time, some of my memories of exact details have faded. There is no doubt that some officers who read this will be able to point out statements that differ somewhat from actual events.

Finally, it should be noted that this book is not a historical documentation of facts. My goal is simply to communicate the various nuances that will bring my stories alive in the most interesting way possible. The ideas expressed in this book are to be taken as *the author's opinion.*

# Introduction

I wrote the following poem for a school literary contest when I was in the eighth grade at Haltom Junior High School. Although it won a measly "honorable mention," it has come to hold more significance for me symbolically than I could ever have imagined at the time:

### Roller Coaster

*In the amusement park, on a warm summer's day*
*The roller coaster sounds this way:*
*With a swoosh it's down the great big hill*
*Around the curve, oh what a thrill;*
*The squeal of the crowd hurts our ears,*
*Because we are sitting at the rear.*
*There's a click, click, click as the coaster climbs,*
*Then back down and around it winds.*
*As the coaster ride ends*
*It's the brakes on which the crowd depends.*
*The end of the ride the coaster has reached;*
*Now the trusty brakes have loudly screeched.*
*As I walk off of that fantastic ride*
*Others are boarding from the other side.*
*As the roller coaster begins to rise –*
*Those people are in for a big SURPRISE!*

Through the eyes of a thirteen year old student in middle school, this poem represents a thrill ride in an amusement park. Conversely, however, through the eyes of a forty year old "student of life," this poem represents peaks and valleys, the slow process of trudging uphill, curvy winding roads, and numerous perspectives life lends from different stages experienced over time. Most significantly, however, it represents the amazing surprises that loom beyond every horizon. Such surprises reveal themselves during those travels along the never ending track of unknown adventures. At the time when I wrote this poem, I didn't realize the significance of the message it held. The implications of the "roller-coaster" metaphor are strikingly parallel to the ups, downs, twists and turns of life for each of us - but most especially for me.

The most gripping observation here is the uncanny correspondence between the roller coaster in my poem and my decision to leave my law enforcement career. As eager thrill-seekers complete their ride, they exit the coaster's protective enclosure, shedding the seatbelt strap and removing the shiny steel bar that has been in place ensuring their preparedness for the upcoming, sometimes brutal effects of the ride. As they disembark, they have untarnished, vivid memories, both pleasant and horrific, of the twists and turns met during the ride. Looking across the chasm now to the other side of the track, they observe a fresh new crew of riders beginning to strap themselves in to the coaster, preparing for the unknown. Finally, that shiny steel bar is positioned strategically across their chest, as the new riders sit confidently waiting for what lies ahead.

While some may choose to walk back around to the place where they can get on again, others will move forward to the next thrilling surprise the park has to offer. This is the choice I had to face after my adventurous ride as a police officer. After fifteen years of strapping on that protective bullet-proof vest and confidently displaying that shiny metal badge across my chest, I recognized that it was time to shed the protective equipment and disembark from the ride of my life. The stripping off of those components that distinctively symbolize the police culture was accompanied by a bittersweet sensation. I found myself simultaneously experiencing a loss of my identity and the retention of my pride. I cannot help but reminisce to my first days of training that were packed with unclear expectations and met with eagerness. This is especially true as I observe the fresh, new groups of candidates entering the classrooms of the academy with their shiny and crisp new gear. They are most certainly in for a big surprise.

I have kept mementos, notes, and journal entries about some

of the incidents I have encountered throughout my career from its very beginning in 1992. However, I only began writing this book while I was on a guard duty detail at a hospital in the summer of 2004. I have continued adding to it periodically over the last several years. Eventually, in July of 2007, I opted for early retirement after my fifteen wonderful years with the Fort Worth Police Department. Even so, my identity as a Fort Worth Officer has become integrated into my soul. I cannot forget my experiences, nor do I want to. It is those experiences which have helped me to grow and to become the person I am today. I feel fortunate and blessed to have had the opportunity to experience so much first hand.

It has become much clearer to me over the past several years that God has a definite design for the life of each of his children. Despite a period in my life when I ignored my Christian beliefs, morals and convictions, I was never ignored by God. He has always been the solid rock of love, forgiveness and provision for me, as He is for all of His children. As I have recognized and accepted this truth as it applies to my life, the abundance of new-found clarity has been remarkable. Consequently, in recent months I have become particularly motivated to complete this project because of the message I hope it will provide for each person who reads it. I pray that the words within will motivate and inspire anyone who questions his or her purpose and direction in life. While I am still travelling that mysterious path the Lord has set before me, I do so with a much more enlightened heart, and that brings me joy. As I said before, I know that my steps are directed, and I have actually seen how this is so. Because of this, I desire to share with you my story of unlikely choices, nearly impossible outcomes, and explicitly divine guidance that has led me through the first forty years of my life.

While working for the Fort Worth Police Department, my life did change for the better in a variety of ways. I learned invaluable life-skills and experienced unique situations that would prepare me for adversity and an ability to cope with almost anything I might encounter in the future. I met remarkable life-long friends who continually bring love and support into my world. Most cherished, however, is the memory of the day I met the handsome patrolman who would one day become my amazing husband. While working the midnight shift in the Traffic Division, I routinely conducted traffic stops for speeding vehicles on North Beach Street. Steve would often roll-up with me to ensure my safety. The first time I met him I noticed his calm, yet assured demeanor. Soon I became mesmerized by his charming personality. Over time I recognized his reputation as an amazing, genuine individual who always exhibited an unmatched level of integrity and respect that was obvious to everyone around him. Most importantly, he made it clear that he was a Christian. This was my kind of guy – someone who would walk alongside me as I tried to get my life back into proper spiritual order. In May of 2008 we celebrated our thirteen-year wedding anniversary. We have had an amazing marriage. Throughout the years I have been continually dumbfounded by the blessing of having Steve as my partner, my best friend, and the love of my life. Although I don't mention him much in the following pages, make no mistake - without Steve, I don't know how I would have made it through the last decade of my life and the daily grind of working through the challenges of my police career.

*This was taken after Steve and me were married in 1995. I was so thankful to meet and marry such an amazing man. God has truly blessed our now thirteen years of marriage!*

Paling in comparison to romance and marriage, yet still profoundly important in my life is the reality that the Department provided a tuition reimbursement benefit for college education. Having missed out on completing a higher education earlier in life due to lack of finances, I took advantage of this benefit to the highest degree possible.

Working full-time with a variety of work shifts and schedules sometimes rendered course-work challenging, but it was worth the effort. As a result of my marathon of persistence that spanned my entire fifteen year career, I received an Associates Degree from Tarrant County College in 2000 and a Bachelor's Degree in Interdisciplinary Studies from Texas Wesleyan University in 2004. Next was my work towards a Master's Degree in Counseling at Texas Wesleyan University in 2006. I transferred in 2007 to a school where I could pursue a more theologically-enriched education. It was during this time that I felt led to become prepared for a more spiritually-sound method of counseling. As a result, I am currently working towards two Master's Degrees at the Southwestern Baptist Theological Seminary in Marriage and Family Counseling and Christian Education. Upon graduation, I hope to work in the counseling field guiding needful clients towards therapeutic change. Thankfully, I am at a stage in my life, now, where I have the desire and the means with which to serve The Lord. I have recently arrived much closer to the place where God has always intended for me to be, and it is here that I give all thanks and glory to Him.

# Chapter One
## Just another Hot Day in Texas

It is a hot, summer, Saturday morning, and for now, I feel lucky. I am getting settled in for a two-hour assignment, and it's a good one. I am sitting here in a nice, cool hospital room with a mental-health patient who is being guarded for attempted suicide. He decided to use a syringe to inject rat-poison mixed with cocaine and heroin into his system. Of course, it must be noted that this young man immediately called 911 to summons an ambulance when the volatile combo began to show its effects. This is an all too common example of someone in need of intervention taking drastic measures to cry out for attention. As a result, Fort Worth Police Officers will spend forty-eight to seventy two hours of police manpower (hu*man*-power that is) in two-hour increments, guarding this man as he drools and snores unconsciously in the bed. He will have to be medically cleared before he can safely and effectively participate in a mental-health evaluation. That means all of the poisons in his system have to be cleansed and metabolized out, which will take awhile. Even though there is no way this poor guy could even walk to the toilet, much less out of the hospital, our orders dictate that we will accompany him through the process until the hospital clears him.

During the resulting downtime, I am sitting here looking at the television. The volume is turned completely down, and I cannot tell exactly what is being said, but it's the local morning news, so narration is really not necessary. I can see that, as usual, the same stories are being repeated from earlier broadcasts. Besides, I have the *Fort Worth Star Telegram* sitting right here on the bed-side table. I glance at the headlines and see nothing that piques my interest. I am already bored. I brought a book

7

to thumb through, but it is just not appealing to me, right now. I fight the urge to giggle when "sleeping beauty" rustles around, restlessly and produces a very loud snorting sound. After fighting back the impulse to laugh out loud, in an attempt to remain somewhat professional, I regain my composure. I begin to feel guilty. This man has enough problems. I should show a little human compassion for him and think for a couple of moments about why he might be here. I have no way of knowing any of his personal anguish, much less his life story. I certainly cannot hold a conversation with him. All I know is that he is in misery, both physically and emotionally. I am watching him writhe in discomfort as poison eats at his body from the inside out and as emotional despair feasts on his mind. I feel juvenile, and reprimand myself for being insensitive and disrespectful. Tears begin to well up in the bottoms of both of my eyes. I whisper a short prayer asking forgiveness. Now it is time to think of something else.

I really thought it would be a treat, being here for two hours. It is only 6:30 a.m., but it is also August in Fort Worth, Texas, and that translates to 90 degrees and a heat-index of much more, upon the rising of the sun, alone. A combination of the heat and our *so-dark-blue-that-it's-almost-black* uniform perpetuates a destructive fusion of heat, lethargy, and an overall draining of the vitality from your very essence. In other words, the Texas heat can suck the life spirit right out of a person. Wearing a nearly black uniform puts a big target on you, guiding the sun's rays on their trek to zap the core of body and soul! In addition, the weight of equipment, leather gear and a ballistic vest adds what seems like at least 25 pounds and 25 degrees to the mere existence of any police officer during a hot day. In spite of that, I suddenly feel the desire to leave this place and take my chances out in the heat. It is not so much the boredom, the sounds, smells and discomfort of the institutional chair that I am sitting in, but more the feeling of my being imprisoned for the actions of another person. That is it, in a nutshell. I want to be able to get up and walk out of here, but I cannot leave my post simply because another person decided to shoot-up rat-poison. How bizarre does that sound? Well to me, not bizarre at all, considering some of the things that I have witnessed first-hand. I realize perhaps I should stop harboring these negative thoughts, and do something worthwhile with my time.

# Chapter Two
## Why Write This Book?

I promised myself that during my career I would keep a journal or at least make notes about the events of my daily life at work. I wanted to document my encounters so that someday I could write a book. I have commonly fielded questions from my friends and relatives who want to hear about my most interesting calls. Further, I have also heard other officers proclaim, "I should write a book," or "my life story about this job would make millions." For me, it is not money that motivates. It is pure, fascination with human nature. It is a phenomenon that has perpetuated thousands of studies, books and social discussions, throughout time. If I had the financial means to attend medical school when I was younger, I probably would have been a psychiatrist. However, after exploring interests in many different fields throughout my life, The Lord has guided me along a particular path, sending me exactly where it was He intended for me to go.

From my little corner of the world there is a very unique perspective. Quite honestly, I believe that any person who might take the time to preserve memories about his or her life could write an interesting book. The mere act of getting out of bed and functioning in society, today, is an accomplishment. The world changes so much, so quickly, and each person defines life in a completely different way. This truth inspires me. People enjoy learning about other people. I enjoy writing, and I always have, so it is my hope that my career highlights might be interesting and entertaining to others. My career would never have been possible if it weren't for the course of events that happened in my life prior to police work. Incidentally, some of those situations became profound learning experiences for me. They involved challenges that, with God's help, I was able to conquer. It is my hope and prayer that my stories will encourage others who might find themselves in similar situations.

Ultimately, however, my most important purpose for this book is the opportunity to show gratitude publicly to my Lord Jesus Christ for His faithful intercession in my life. I want my experiences of His faithfulness and love to serve as inspiration to those who might be feeling a lack of direction in life. I realized very late in my life that God had a special path for me to travel. I felt for awhile as if it were too late for me to do what I felt led to do. I felt trapped, and didn't know how to move out into the realm of the unknown.

I fought God's direction regularly and vigorously. Over time, however, His gentle prodding turned into a slightly more pronounced nudge. Then it evolved into a high-powered collision with my will. This divine collision eventually changed the direction of my life. Only after I ignored those subtle indications, and had to be practically slapped into submission by God did I realize that He wanted me to move for Him. When I finally surrendered, He provided the way and the means. This simply involved my stepping out onto that new pathway with faith. This path led me to a forum where I would find pure fascination and awe.

There are so many people in this world, so many cultures, expectations and norms that we integrate into our everyday lives. My career as a police officer has opened my eyes to facets of society that I never realized existed, until my own personal encounters. I know that police dramas are popular viewing on television. I also know that cable networks today cater successfully to public interest in law-enforcement. Why? I think it's because law-enforcement, by its mere nature, provides windows through which we can look into every-day lives of real people. These are the same people that some of us desire to, and all of us *need to* learn more about.

Realistically, I am spotlighting the City of Fort Worth, a medium-to-large sized city in the remarkable State of Texas, in the United States of America. Abstractly, however, I am presenting to you a unique view of one person's life that has been changed by the incredible environment that can be found within a 345 square mile chunk of this world. The thing that makes my view different is the very fact that it is *my view*. Although there is only one of "me" scrambling around here on this earth I have realized how profoundly God has intervened in my random, seemingly insignificant life. He has made me feel loved, and I am honored to be a special creation of His. This book is an opportunity to give praise to God. If I failed to document some of the things I have experienced, this opportunity would be overlooked. Ultimately, I would be ashamed if I neglected to share the testimony of some of the remarkable interventions God has performed in my life. He is awesome!

# Chapter Three
## The Beginning - How an Unlikely Police Career Became a Reality

During the course of just over fifteen years of police-work, I thoroughly enjoyed recounting events that occurred during my work shifts. These stories, referred to as "war stories," have proven to fascinate my friends and family time and time again. Several important people in my life even joined me for a ride-along to see for themselves. When my stories became real, the whole idea fueled their fascination. When the depth of my shy nature, my ambivalence and my lack of athleticism came to light, it was glaringly clear how God must have had a sense of humor, sending me to the Fort Worth Police Department.

Throughout the years as I have provided play-by-play details about exciting calls, my friends and relatives have a hard time placing me in the picture. When I verbalize these stories, it's not just "an officer" who arrested someone for robbery, but instead, "Kelly?" "Quiet, shy, Kelly arrested a robber? No way! Tell me about it!" Now I am a retired fifteen year veteran of the Fort Worth Police Department. The reality of my career choice was perplexing for my friends and family because around twenty five years ago, I was a high-school journalist on the school newspaper staff who was mortified by the thought of approaching and interviewing a football player for a story. I was extremely shy and had no self-confidence.

I am an only child who was over-protected by my parents during my entire childhood. I was eventually able to break out of my shell and I worked hard toward the goal of catching up on my social skill deficit. Never, though, did anyone around me think that I would someday don a police uniform. It's not that they *didn't think I could do it*; but it is more that they *didn't know I wanted to.*

Amazingly enough, I didn't really know that I wanted to, myself, until one day when I decided to put in an application to the Fort Worth Police Department, just because they were hiring. I honestly did not expect to hear back from them. I just knew that they would not be interested in a pharmaceutical data-entry clerk who had work experience as an executive assistant and as a cosmetician at a local drug store. I wasn't a military veteran or a life-long passionately aspiring police officer. I was simply a typical twenty-three year old who was bored with my current job, and who needed a change.

## My Own Domestic Hell
*[This story depicts violence, drug and alcohol use]*

In all actuality, however, I did have a hidden, subconscious fascination with police work. I had, after all, lived through a series of traumatic experiences throughout which the Haltom City Police Department and many of its officers had been of the utmost help to me. I guess, deep down, my admiration for them turned into a quest to repay such kindnesses with my own service to the community. Through a twisted series of events, I learned the value of law enforcement protection in a way that I hope others never have to experience. The following segment will enlighten you as to the foolish choices I made some twenty years ago that eventually led to my high regard for the protective duties of law enforcement officers.

I was twenty years old when a friend introduced me to the young man that would become my first husband. He was a casual acquaintance whom she did not know well, but he seemed nice enough. This guy was very charming, attentive, and was always available to spend time with me. We quickly (much too quickly) developed a relationship and I fell in love with the attention he gave me. I thought I was in love with him. I craved the attention, and I so desperately wanted to be married that I ignored several red flags and warning signs. I was very immature, and did not have my priorities established, yet. I cast aside considerations of all of the important qualities necessary for a suitable life-partner, like godliness, maturity, morals and wisdom. I did not even think to consider evaluating

14

him as a spiritual leader of our soon to be household, even though I was a Christian. At this time, I did not give regard to the wisdom I had been taught during my life, nor did I listen to the quiet, yet sovereign prompting from the Holy Spirit in my heart. I ignored God, and made my own choices. It was what *I* wanted to do. We met in December of 1988, and we impulsively married in June of 1989.

In addition to the many other red flags, I also disregarded the fact that this man drank beer regularly and that he smoked cigarettes. Inside I was secretly hoping he would quit drinking and smoking. I even overlooked the fact that he had quit school. He claimed he wanted to get his G.E.D. (diploma equivalency) so he could better support a family. I failed to acknowledge all of this, and much more, because I simply desired to have a partner in my life. I was looking in the wrong place for companionship and love. I did not know this man nearly as well as I thought I did. He fooled a lot of people. He acted charming around everyone, but inside, he had hidden demons.

On the day of our wedding, he turned into a monster. He acted as if he thought I was finally "his" forever! I detected a change in him immediately. It was as if he let out a big sigh of relief and the demons inside of him shed their misleadingly charming facade. He let his true personality manifest that day. The change in him was very surprising to me. It was a tangible transformation accompanied by enraged, piercing eyes, a red face, swollen veins in his forehead, and a clenched fist. I was in total shock because it happened so quickly. Sadly, it happened within two hours after our wedding. When we left the church on our way to San Antonio for our honeymoon, he yelled at me for being hungry and refused to stop for food. I had not been able to eat because I was too nervous during the wedding and reception. I had only had a bite of our wedding cake during the posed shots for our photography. All I wanted was to roll through a drive-thru at a fast-food restaurant and grab a bite. He cursed at me, told me that I was stupid for not eating, and refused to stop. At that point, I wondered what I had gotten into. I felt a sickening feeling in the pit of my stomach. I realized I had made a big mistake. *This was the day of my wedding.* It was supposed to be the happiest day of my life. Unfortunately, I had just embarked upon my worst nightmare.

Before a week had passed, the honeymoon was over. Upon our arrival back home to our apartment our wedding photos were waiting for us. My friend came to see them while my new husband was at work. He was one of my best friends from high-school who had been an usher for us. He came over with his mom, excited to see how well our pictures had turned out, partially because he was in many of them. When my husband got home, I told him my friend had been there. He became enraged and irrationally jealous. He told me to *never* let another man in our home when he wasn't there. He called me a whore. He picked up the phone and called my friend and told him to never speak to me again. This was one of my best friends. My friend was shocked, and when I called him later to apologize, he would not talk to me. He hung up the phone immediately. He must have thought we were both crazy.

This friend was someone I had spent a lot of time with for three years during high school. He had been like a brother to me. Before I met my new husband we constantly ran around together. We would see movies together and go out to eat. We would sometimes just drive around and sing our lungs out in the car. Our relationship was nothing inappropriate. It was, however a very special and fulfilling friendship. He was one of the best friends I could have ever wished for. I lost the magic of his friendship that day. Even after later attempts to apologize there was still tension between us for years. Memories of the strain our relationship suffered still cause the pit of my stomach to twist miserably. It is a sickening feeling. We have since reconciled, but I shudder at the thought of how he was treated, and how things could have been different if he had not been insulted by this irrational man I married.

Even though I could detect some nearly insurmountable problems forthcoming in my new marriage, I felt committed to stay, due to the "for better or worse, in sickness and in health" vows I had taken. I considered the possibility that my new husband had a mental illness. I vowed to take care of him. It was my choice to marry him, and I had made it hastily. Now I felt I must learn to live with it even though he was acting irrational, immature, possessive, jealous, violent, and very distrusting. I had never given him any reason to distrust me, but he constantly accused me of lying, sneaking, and being deceitful towards him. Perhaps he felt guilty about his own demons and deceitful behaviors.

He would leave to go "wash his car" every Sunday and would inevitably return to pick a fight about things which were so insignificant I cannot recall even one of them, and I lived through nine-months of them.

Furthermore, when he came home, he always smelled like marijuana. He said it was because his friends at the car wash were all smoking marijuana, but he was absolutely not smoking it. I so badly wanted to believe him that I let my own denial blind me. I asked him to stop hanging around those people. He told me he wouldn't. I needed to trust him. He began playing mind games with me. He spent time with his friends who would smoke drugs and drink alcohol constantly. I had to give up almost all of my long-time friends. When I didn't, he would do it himself by making one of his threatening phone calls to them.

Every Sunday night he would go for that "car wash" and would arrive home with an irresistible urge to fight and argue. I would try so hard to avoid a fight. I thought his temper was due to his intoxication. He always became very violent when he drank beer. Every time, without fail, he would start an argument out of the blue, about nothing of importance whatsoever. He often came home cursing and throwing things. In one instance he threw our cordless phone, piercing a gaping hole in a hollow apartment door. During another argument, he poured a hot dishpan full of water over my head. Still another time he took all of my clothes from the closet and ripped them up. Afterwards he threw them on the floor and stomped on them. Once he had a baseball bat in the apartment, and held it up like he was going to hit me. I truly thought I was going to die. I could see those demons in his eyes. Instead, surprisingly, he hit himself in the head with the bat repeatedly. He was completely out of control. Then he fell into the corner of the room and rolled up into a ball in a fetal position and started crying. He said he was sorry, and realized he needed to work on his temper. I did not tell my parents because I did not want them to know how badly I had screwed up. I lived in fear, dread and misery every day, for months.

There were times when I caught him following me to the grocery store, mall, school, and work to watch me. He tried to act like he was "just in the area" although the logic behind that was completely absent. He made no sense at all. I was scared to death of him. I lived every day knowing I had ruined my life. During one Sunday evening argument I left the house for groceries to allow him time to cool off. He didn't want me to go. I went anyway, knowing I had to get away, even if only for a few minutes. He followed me and circled around as I looked for a parking space. When I turned onto a row of parked vehicles and began to drive down the aisle, he faced off against me from the opposite end of the parking lot. He accelerated like he was preparing for a drag race, and proceeded to violently ram my car, head on. Luckily, God was watching over me that day. Neither of us was seriously hurt, although both of our cars had sustained serious damage. As I sat in the parking lot and tried to regain my composure, I quickly realized we would need help in order to get both vehicles home.

I called my parents and lied to them. It was one of the most painful things I have ever had to do. I told them in a roundabout way that it was an accident, and somehow they believed me. This incident cost us a lot of money which we didn't have. Once we arrived home, he rolled up in the fetal position in the corner, crying and begging me to forgive him and give him another chance. He pleaded and acted like a child. I stayed with him, mainly because I felt I had to. I truly believed he was mentally ill and needed help. We now faced more hardships because both of our vehicles were ruined. We were short on money to begin with, and now had to borrow money for a new car.

He always charmed my parents. I lied to them, so they never knew anything was wrong. Our Sunday night fights continued and escalated. He drank and then came home smelling like smoke. Not just cigarette smoke, but marijuana smoke. I quickly learned what that smelled like. It was very distinctive. He denied using it. It was always only his friends who were smoking. During one fight, I tried to leave. He wouldn't let me leave our apartment, again. I didn't have it in me to go through another argument. I tried to walk out of the front door of the apartment. He grabbed me, and I held on to the door facing with both hands. I was in the front doorway, pulling against him. I was trying to get out. He was trying to keep me in. He picked me up like a wheelbarrow and dropped me from four feet up the door facing. I landed on the threshold and busted my lip and the inside of my mouth. I yelled out to our neighbors to call the police. They were so used to us fighting that they ignored me. I could see them watching us out the window, but no one made a move to help me. It was my own fault, because this went on every single week, and I stayed there. They assumed that it was our normal weekly fight, although it was escalating, quickly. When I fell, and was bleeding, my husband ran out of the apartment.

I got up and went next door to a neighbor's to use the phone.

They didn't want to let me in, but I was bleeding, crying, and my clothes were torn. After I begged them and convinced them that he was gone, they finally let me in. I called a friend's mom, and she let me come over. I was very scared that he would come back to the apartment and actually kill me.

Monday mornings always seemed like I was living an entirely different life in a completely different world. I would get up, attempt to disguise my red and puffy eyes, drink some caffeinated beverage to give me the energy to move, and go to work, just like nothing had ever happened. My husband went to work, too. During each of his breaks, he would call to say he was sorry, and I would go back home at the end of the day, as always. During our arguments and fights he never actually hit me, but he did everything else you could imagine to hurt me. I prayed that I would just survive from day to day. Even so, I somehow felt that I deserved what I was living because of my poor choices. I felt compelled to stay in the marriage, because I knew that I had made a commitment. I was a Christian, and I wanted to do the right thing and keep my vows to my husband. Inside, I realized things had to change quickly or I would surely end up dead. Sometimes I thought that dying wouldn't be so bad. While it may be painful, it would mean an end to the constant hurt, fear and dread which now consumed me. I wasn't mature and did not know where to turn. By instinct from my childhood in Sunday school, I prayed for guidance.

One day, after about six months of marriage, my husband was out with a friend, as usual. I went to look in his truck for a hammer to hang a picture that had fallen during one of our fights. I pulled the seat forward. There was a large gallon-sized clear plastic baggie full of marijuana behind the seat. A rush of emotion went through my whole body. I was infuriated at first. I could have been driving that truck. If a police officer had pulled me over for any little thing, I could have been arrested. It was such a large amount that it would have scarred my record for life. The police never would have believed that I was unaware of it. I was mortified, but I also became very hurt in my heart. It was such a shock to me, and my mind could not solidify any emotion for very long. I felt like I was being tossed around in a tornado, but I was standing still.

Then, as quickly as the shock had set in, an amazing and all encompassing peacefulness came over me. I had an idea that this may be my ticket out of this mess. I suddenly felt like this was an answer to my prayers, straight from God. Logically, I suspected that the drugs were his. As a result, it became clear that if they were, then my husband's irrational and violent behaviors were the direct result of his choice to use mind-altering drugs. My surprise discovery of this illegal substance gave me something tangible to hold on to. I heard the still, small voice of the Holy Spirit telling me to use this as my reason to get out of this marriage. I knew that God did not want me to stay. He had listened to my pleadings. He was going to have mercy on my poor, ignorant soul, and He was going to lead me out of this dangerous and tangled mess. God was giving me an "out."

I felt very afraid to get a divorce. At first, I had an overwhelming feeling that I would become a substandard individual if I got a divorce. I felt that it would ruin my life. Somehow, divinely, I began to feel calmness within my soul. It was a peace that God gave me. Eventually, I felt in my heart that it was going to be okay. I had sinned by entering into this marriage against the advice of God. Now that I was listening to Him, He was going to guide me through a safe escape. Just as He had always done before, He was going to direct my path through this difficult process. Even though I felt ashamed, I would rather be divorced than dead. I believe even now that if I had remained in that marriage, I would no longer be alive. Ultimately, I knew I would be forgiven for my divorce, and the peacefully prodding voice of the Holy Spirit was encouraging me to escape this dangerous lifestyle.

I used a rather creative approach in order to secure the drugs in a safe place while I figured out what other actions to take. I took the bag, wrapped it in foil, and labeled it "hamburger meat." Afterward, I put it in our freezer inside the apartment. When my husband was dropped off at home by his friend, I told him that I had found the large bag of drugs in his truck. He became enraged. The demon in him came out. His voice changed and he began to sweat profusely. He asked me where the bag was. His veins were popping out. He became such a monster. He yelled and approached me and got right in my face and demanded them back. I bluffed him by telling him that they were no longer in the apartment. I told him that I had given them to someone. I further warned that the person who had them was aware of the fact that I was going to confront him, and if he touched me, the police would be contacted. Luckily he fell for it.

I told him that I finally understood why we had so many problems, and that I wanted a divorce immediately. I told him that if he would take his stuff and leave, I would not report the drugs to police. He went ballistic and came towards me. I reminded him that if he touched me, the person who had the marijuana would call the police. They would know what happened because I had already warned them he would be mad. Basically, I completely tricked him. I was the only person on earth who knew that the marijuana was in our freezer. I really didn't want to tell anyone about it. I was ashamed, and didn't want to admit it. I knew that if I had given him access to it when I confronted him, he would have destroyed it. He would have found a way to scare me into staying. I was not going to give up my only chance to get out of there! I made it clear to him that I would not tolerate drugs. Seemingly defeated, he packed some things and left.

I put up a great front to scare him away. The entire time, though, I was frightened beyond words. Thankfully, he was afraid of the police. He went to his parents' house and called me from there. He begged for another chance, but I would not hear of it. I filed for divorce. He came back with his dad to get his clothes and some furniture a couple of days later.

Within a month of our split, I got my credit card bill, which had originally been in my name before we were married. When we got married, he had no credit cards. I gave him a duplicate card from my account to use for emergencies. I found that in the course of one month, he had charged up $1,200. He had been using it to *charge* fuel, food, cigarettes and beer for all of his friends in exchange for drugs. I didn't have a clue how I would pay for that. That was an incredible amount of money. Luckily the people I worked for let me do odd jobs for them, and paid me generously. They paid me to iron clothes, baby-sit, clean house, rake leaves and even clean pools. The Lord gave me a test, a struggle, but he also gave me the means to conquer it. With His help, and the generosity of some good people, I paid off the credit card within several months. I didn't argue with my husband about possessions so our divorce process would move swiftly. He ended up taking all of the furniture, which had been a birthday gift to us from my parents.

I kept that bag of frozen drugs in the freezer for a long time. It served a purpose as a form of protection for me. It was something to hang over his head, a type of insurance. He couldn't stand not being in control of me. I was like a possession that he had lost.

One night he came to my apartment while I was living there alone during our divorce. He banged on the door. I wouldn't let him in. He broke out my window. I called 911 and I locked myself in my bathroom, while I braced myself to die. I've never been more afraid in my life. It was like the scariest horror movie ever, and I was living it. I just knew that if he made it in, he would kill me. I had the dispatcher on the phone with me. She heard him yelling and banging and the glass breaking. I heard her tell officers to speed it up. She even sounded shaken up. I heard sirens, and then my now estranged husband's tires screeching as he sped away. Thankfully he had heard the sirens. He was never caught that day after the police scared him away. This was the first time I had ever actually called police during seven months of violent fighting and abuse.

## "Protect and Serve" A Different Perspective

After that episode, the officers in Haltom City began to routinely sit in the church parking lot across the street from my apartment and complete their paperwork. I can remember the feeling of peace and comfort I felt as I would peek out the blinds and see the patrol car sitting there. The mere presence of someone there, as a protector, restored my equilibrium back to the point in my life where I could function without sheer terror. My estranged husband left me alone for a good while after that, because he knew that I would not hesitate to call for help, and he knew I still had the bag of marijuana hidden away somewhere.

Eventually, a lifelong friend moved in with me. I was feeling safer, as time passed. For unknown reasons, my soon-to-be-ex-husband started to stalk me and watch me again. My roommate was even forced to endure his creepy behavior as he followed us to the mall and other places we would frequent. He was everywhere. He followed us to school at Tarrant County Junior College where my friend and I were taking a class together. Eventually, I realized that I would have to make drastic changes in order to be safely rid of him. I was reluctantly forced to leave my job where I had been happily employed for several years. He was calling, coming to my place of employment, and threatening me far too often. My coworkers were being put in danger, and my reputation was being damaged by his stalking and the seemingly psychotic behavior he continually exhibited. Thankfully, the Lord provided me with another great job. I found that He provided for me when I needed it. I had learned to have faith that with His help, I could break away from this stalking nightmare. My roommate and I left the current apartment. I moved to another nearby city with a different female friend. With my new job, I was able to get my first ever brand new car. It was small, but it was safe and reliable. I did not visit my parents for a very long time so that he would not follow me there. I quit going to my lifelong church, so he would not find me and bring trouble there. I continued to attend my classes, but I parked on the opposite side of the campus in my new car. I always ran into the building, hoping he would never recognize me. After about six months of this, I finally felt like I had survived, and I felt safe again. When he couldn't find me, he gave up. Eventually the divorce process was completed, and it was finally over.

This was such a traumatic time in my life. Unfortunately, it had spanned nine long and miserable months. In the timeline of my life, however, it was just a little tick of the clock. I have not seen or heard from this man now for well over eighteen years. The adversities I was forced to face during this nearly year-long period of terror have helped me through numerous situations as a police officer. I have been able to encourage battered women from a perspective of having been there. I have often refused to accept excuses from victims simply because, in my opinion, there is not an acceptable excuse for staying in a violent and dangerous relationship. If there were an acceptable one out there, I surely would have perfected it myself when I was in the same position.

After extensive growing and maturing over the course of the next three years of my life, I finally took to heart what I had always been taught in Sunday school. Jesus loved me, and I was forgiven. I had asked Jesus into my heart when I was a teenager. I had been baptized, and I knew that I was saved. Despite the fact that I often heard the voice of the Holy Spirit in my heart, for that current season of my life I had been ignoring Him. Now I recognized, however, that God did something incredible for me by leading me out of my imprisonment in that domestic violence situation. How could I waste a second chance to make something of myself? It was this realization that prompted me to try harder to become a successful person. At this point in my life, even though I was feeling victorious over adversity, I did still not give the credit to Whom it was due, at least not yet. Apparently I needed more convincing before I would change my ways.

Over time, it became clear that my social skills deficit resulting from my adolescent bashfulness began to turn into a surplus of desire for social interaction. As a result, I often had to bite my tongue at work in the office environment to keep from getting in trouble for talking too much. I needed some freedom to roam about, and to socialize. It seemed that I should be looking for a job where I could do this and get paid for it - because I was good at it! My mind and mouth were making up for about twenty-years of shyness and now I was ready to interact with the world. Much to my complete amazement and my parent's complete terror, The Department accepted me as a candidate for the police academy.

## The Great City of Fort Worth

Now that you know *how* I got into this position, let me tell you about what happened once I got here. This book contains stories and accounts of actual people, places and events that I have experienced throughout my career. To me and my fellow officers these everyday occurrences have become routine and sometimes non-eventful. However, we are still regularly taken aback, often amused, and occasionally, scared beyond words. However, when I stop and think about how some of these things probably sound to people who are not officers, I can't even begin to predict a reaction.

These accounts of my experiences are organized into different categories. They reflect my academy experience, training periods, dangerous, disturbing, and tragic calls, as well as some of the unbelievably creative messes people can sometimes become involved in (myself included). Many of these situations lend themselves to humor, while many others are gut-wrenching and dismal.

Before I proceed further, I will attempt to provide you with an accurate picture of the City in which I have served. It might be helpful for you as the reader to have some background information about the demographics of Fort Worth. At the time I began writing this book, according to the City of Fort Worth's official web site, its population is approximately 686,850. The racial makeup is approximately 44% Caucasian, 18% African American, 32% Hispanic and 6% other races.

My personal observation has been that the socio-economical demographics of this city span a scope from the homeless and transient to the incredibly wealthy and affluent. The focus will not be upon racial or economic status of the citizens in my references to them. Even so, I want to assure you that my dealings with the citizens of our City have been as diverse and unique as the demographics portrayed above. It is necessary for you as the reader to understand the overall size and makeup of Fort Worth in order to appreciate, completely, the events portrayed on the following pages.

In essence, the City of Fort Worth embodies the personality of cultural and economic patchwork where many different types of people co-exist and strive towards their dreams in their respective lifestyles. It is not easy to look at any one person on the street and tell whether that dream is to find a meal for the evening's dinner, a shelter with running water, make it to a child's soccer game, attend a political fundraiser or to purchase a sports franchise.

Diversity is an integral part of the amazing mystique of Fort Worth. Each individual is just that. They *are* individual. However, in being such, each person is a crucial component of the perfect balance that makes our City great. Please do not mistakenly presume that I am being disrespectful or making fun of the people whose stories are included here. Furthermore, know that I do not take anyone's misery or despair lightly. I have cultivated an incredible amount of compassion for the people involved in the events I will describe to you. Before you become angry with how officers sometimes deal with the circumstances they face, I appeal to you to grasp how it must feel to deal with acute crises on a regular basis. Think about how difficult it must be to keep a well-adjusted view of society without becoming biased. Think of the different types of self-preservation techniques that must be used to help officers cope with disturbing events. There is a tremendous amount of mental and physical stress as well as self-discipline required of police officers. This is especially true as they undertake the variety of tasks that are necessary for the fulfillment of expected duties. It is a difficult requirement, but those of us who have taken the oath to protect and serve manage to do just that. The protection, however, must also extend to the officer in the name of self-preservation. This is in order for officers to remain competent and capable to serve in the face of unpredictable circumstances.

My point is this: Although I am writing about events that involve all types of people, I respect each of them as citizens to whom I have given my best as an honest and fair public servant. This book is not written with disregard or disrespect for anyone. It is, on the contrary, a tribute to the human race, and more specifically, to the members of the human race who live in the City of Fort Worth.

# Chapter Four
## The Academy

The whole concept of me being in the police academy was rather comical. My parents were both mortified. They were very proud and supportive, but I also believe that they were in some state of shock, as well. They just waited to see what would happen. I don't know if they really thought I would complete the academy and actually graduate. That was an extremely valid consideration, because they knew me very well. Even so, God's plan for my life prevailed, and I made it through.

### Physical Training

Sometimes I too wondered if I would be able to satisfactorily complete the academy's requirements. This was true, especially, when I began to participate in the daily physical training regimen, which was essentially the most rigorous physical exertion I have ever experienced. We had a routine of sixty sit ups and sixty push ups every day, after our class run that ranged from a mile-and-a-half to three-miles. We were running our longest runs in June and July, when the humidity and temperature rendered the air oppressively hot.

As we picked up the pace at about the one-mile mark during those daily excursions, I remember the feeling that I could not take another step. The mere existence of "me" was too much weight to carry in the humid heat, and I was exhausted. I weighed about 165 pounds, but during the run I felt as if I weighed twice as much and more. It wasn't unusual for me to yell out during our daily class run, "Oh Lord, help me, or let me die!" I had several classmates who would push me from behind, and some who would grab my arm and pull me along.

In my case, I was blessed with a group of class members who did not ridicule me (too my face, anyway) and who did not label me "inferior" because of my difficulties. I had never been an athlete, but my heart was in it, and now that I had been selected to represent Fort Worth as an officer, I wanted to do a good job. As a matter of fact, I wanted to do a superior job, but I was just not made to run three miles a day, as was evidenced by my loudly-voiced appeals for divine intervention. Consequently, even today my fellow officers who were in class with me won't let me forget the boldly proclaimed prayers I regularly yelled out loud during those class runs.

## Empathy Training

I was joined in my appeals to the Higher Power, however, when we had to maneuver the tear gas tower! The academy staff thought we needed to fully empathize with anyone we might later decide to spray with our pepper spray. As a result, they sent us up about six-stories of stairs in the fire training tower and let the teargas flow. We had to run through it to get down out of the tower. When we got to the bottom, everyone stood around crying, snorting, sniffing, and coughing. When we finally opened our eyes, we wanted to quickly close them again because the pain was only exacerbated by the contact with air (and the sight of everyone else around us standing with a three-foot train of snot hanging out of each nostril).

I guess we were lucky back then. Currently in the academy everyone has to get sprayed directly in the face with a highly-concentrated pepper spray. They also have to get zapped with a Taser. I am thankful that the Taser was not invented when I was in the academy! I also remember being thankful that the academy staff did not feel the need to have us experience the feeling of being shot with our .357 Smith and Wesson revolver they would be issuing to us upon our graduation!

## Punching-Pact that Packed a Punch

If they didn't kill those of us who were not athletically inclined with physical training each day, they tried to weed out the lightweights in other more creative ways. For instance, each of us was paired up with someone of comparable size and weight in the gym for a boxing match. As I have insisted before, I have never been an athlete - and I have certainly never been a fighter. I was not accustomed in any manner to what it would take to box someone and not get knocked out immediately. As a result, my partner and I consulted before the match. We decided that we would hold back a bit when we were up. We agreed to slack off a bit, but to make it look like we were really hitting hard, so we didn't hurt one another.

Well, I held up my part of the bargain, but after a couple of easy connections between she and I, my partner knocked me with all of her might in the diaphragm, and I lost all of my breath in one huge cough of air. I tried to remain standing and continue our "mock fight," but I began to feel both lightheadedness and dizziness, and as a result, I fell backward, hitting the ground. I was knocked out from her gut-punch. Again, I felt I must be the biggest idiot that had ever applied to work for the Fort Worth Police Department. After a chance to regain my breath, I had to get back up and resume the fight. I remember initially being angry with my partner, but I did not have the strength or the ability to hit her back as effectively as she had hit me. Even as humiliating as it was, that boxing exercise was a great lesson for me. I realized my weakness in the area of fighting, which was the main point of the exercise. This realization allowed me to understand what it would be like out in the real world, where if I fell on my back, someone would be in a much better position to finish me off. I survived the day, and as a result, I survived my fifteen years. As for my partner who broke our pact – I guess she was instrumental in teaching me a different type of lesson than the ones intended by the academy staff – don't ever trust a girl in boxing gloves!

**Zoomos**

There were other events during the course of the academy which brought needless misery and utter humiliation to the candidates. There was an ingenuitive type of punishment that was akin to the "time-out" penalty for small children. For adult cadets, this consisted of running in circles while the rest of the class watched. This humiliation tool was called the "zoomo." Zoomos were the punishment that brought the highest level of disgrace to candidates. Being sentenced to them meant utter shame and embarrassment, as well as an incredible inconvenience. This is because in the hottest part of the day in June, the recipients, who would be decked out in the starched, long-sleeved academy uniforms (which reminded us of bus driver uniforms), would be running a certain number of laps around the inside of the pistol range. If someone walked on the grass, zoomos were given. If someone forgot to pick up all of his or her shell casings, they ran zoomos. If all of the equipment was not restored to its proper condition, zoomos were handed out to the guilty party. Those who ran zoomos just helped to motivate the rest of us to follow all of the guidelines when we were out at the range.

Unfortunately, the concept of "positive peer pressure" was impressed upon our class on at least one occasion, with regard to zoomos. As a result, we all suffered for the transgressions of one of our loud-mouthed colleagues. We were sitting in class at about 2:30 in the afternoon on a hot, June day. This cadet decided to argue with one of our guest instructors about the accuracy of his statements while he was teaching. Before we all knew it, the entire class was lined up in front of the academy doors, facing out onto Calvert Street. We were instructed to run a zoomo from the front door of the academy to the intersection of Calvert and Henderson Street. It was ridiculously hot, and we were in our uniforms that required a lot of ironing to get that crease just right for inspection. By the time we were done, the uniforms were all soaking wet, and in need of another laundering. Everyone in the entire class threatened to send this student our cleaning bills for the week. I am not sure exactly what transpired in the men's locker room on the next break after our 105 degree afternoon jog, but after this particular day that individual did not challenge an instructor again.

## Pork Chop Squad

I survived that phase of training, but my lack of athleticism was further evidenced by my assignment to what was called the "pork chop squad." This was the group of candidates whose body fat percentage was above an acceptable level. We were just barely accepted for the academy based on other more desirable factors, but our physical fitness status became a matter of "get in shape – or get out." As a result, we had to log in our daily food intake and do extra exercises. I did not mind this; it was a great opportunity for me to improve my health.

30

I did, however, take issue with one of the academy staff members who would come in with a big smile on his face every day during our lunch. Don't get me wrong, it was not a smile of kindness. It was, instead, an extremely evil and wicked smile. This guy would relentlessly peruse each of our lunch bags, showing great satisfaction as he evaluated each item carefully. After his pillaging episode, he would confiscate and discard every one of our beloved snacks and desserts that were not fruit!

During the academy, I shopped carefully for low-fat and low-sugar items, and I balanced my diet according to my goal of losing weight while maintaining my energy level. A part of this plan for me included chocolate. I *needed* my chocolate! On one particular occasion, I remember this individual looking into my bag and pulling out my low fat chocolate cream-filled cupcake. This cupcake was important to me! As a matter of fact, at the time, it was what I lived for. It was the only chocolate I was allowing myself to eat during the academy, and I looked forward to it in the midst of a physically and mentally stressful day. Despite my sentiments for my chocolate cupcake, the dessert Gestapo took it from me and threw it, with much fervor, into the large fifty-gallon trash can. Two things went through my mind simultaneously. One was my evaluation of whether or not I could dive into the trash can and get my cupcake without getting my uniform dirty, and the second was self-talk in the way of personal restraint - holding me back from throwing oranges and apples at this guy. Both thoughts were abandoned after only a few seconds. The loss of my chocolate had rendered me temporarily delirious, and despite my need for that celebrated dessert, I quickly redirected my brain to the reality that I needed my job more than I needed that cupcake.

Because of this disturbing development, I learned that in order to properly secure my chocolate fix each day, I had to resort to hiding my cupcakes in my gym bag. Because I was a female, that evil man could not come into the locker room and raid my locker! Apparently female staff members understood the need for chocolate, so thankfully, I was safe. I didn't feel the least bit guilty running into that secret room during break time to take a bite of that luscious creamy cupcake. I just had to be sure to wipe the brown crumbs off of my uniform before emerging into the hallway upon my return to class. Over time it became clear that I had become victorious over the dessert Gestapo. I had prevailed with the comforting truth that my chocolate was available when I needed it.

Being a member of the "pork chop squad" was obviously not an aspiration or an esteemed accomplishment. As a matter of fact, it was our job as officers in training to be removed from the group as soon as possible. For me, that meant a lot of extra work with my diet, as well as in the physical fitness department. As a result, I spent extra hours in the academy gym, lifting weights, doing leg presses, sit ups, and running on the treadmill or riding the stationary bicycle. There was even a group of us who would meet on Saturday mornings to ride our bikes for several miles down the trails through Trinity Park.

I had a twofold goal for working out so diligently. First, I intended to build up muscle mass in my legs so that I could make the runs. Secondly, I needed to burn off fat and lose weight so I could carry myself on the runs. It was the hardest work I have ever had to do, but I did so in fear of losing my job. At least that was my motivation at first. However, once I began to notice the difference in my energy level, muscle tone, and performance with the class, it became much more than fear that motivated me. It was now more the sense of satisfaction that I had broken through a personal wall that had been such a stubborn obstacle. I was actually trimming down, toning up, and eventually, I was able to keep up with the class. I was able to finish the physical aspects of the academy without any further problems.

Even after I was removed from the "pork chop squad" I was still very cautious about my diet, and continued to do my extra running and exercises. The Fort Worth Police Department had accomplished the first step in a transformation process which converted me into a candidate who was a bit more suitable for becoming an officer in this fine City.

## Humiliation
*[This story may be offensive due to content regarding sexual assault]*

I was one of only four female trainees in Class #85. As I said before, my gender did not have any detrimental effects on my treatment. I felt accepted and trusted by my classmates. As a matter of fact, they elected me to be the Vice-President of our class. Even after my immense struggle with the physical training regimen (made successful by the support of my very team-oriented fellow-classmates) I made it through the process, one day and one week at a time. Academics have always been a strong point for me, so I was able to do quite well on the examinations regarding the Penal Code, Traffic laws, Code of Criminal Procedures, officer safety, and the FWPD General Orders. We had a test almost every Friday, and I usually did quite well.

However, academic ability is only a very small part of one's suitability for police work. There are numerous facets of a person that must be cultivated and fine-tuned before entering the community. Behind physical training, there was another aspect of the academy that was especially hard for me to grasp. That was practical application of concepts to real-life situations. One particularly excruciating example was the report-writing phase of training. During this learning module our instructor was a very well-accomplished detective. He chose members of our class to join him up on the stage to role-play situations that we would undoubtedly experience at some point during our actual field-work.

During the course of his instruction, it was made known that I was very shy, I still somewhat lacked self-confidence, and I did not like to use profanity. As a result, this detective, who was known for his undying quest for humor at the expense of others, chose me to be the reporting officer. As I approached the stage, a bit nervous already for having to think fast and be evaluated in front of my peers, he began to act out a scenario that was nearly impossible to handle with any semblance of dignity. He assumed the character of a homosexual man who had been raped, and who was in utter despair. He was using profanity to describe the incident, all the while bursting into screaming, crying and carrying-on just as many complaining victims often do. Although this exercise was representative of a potentially real and serious scenario, this man's dramatics were grossly exaggerated, which resulted in the class breaking out into uncontrollable laughter. Despite the distractions of the laughter in the room, I was standing up there in front of everyone, expected to deal with this "complainant" in a respectful, courteous manner. It was my job to calm him enough to gather the pertinent information to make an accurate report.

After our instructor stopped his rant for this scenario, I was asked provide an account of the reported incident verbally to the detective to ascertain whether or not I had obtained sufficient information about the crime. His dissertation obviously included numerous sexual acts, slang terms for body parts and countless expletives, along with the description of the suspect and other necessary details. I was mortified to be standing in front of the class faced with that difficult situation that was further complicated by the instructor and his dramatics. His simulated "victim" had provided me with way too much, way too graphic information! Needless to say, the members of my class got their laugh-ration for the entire week from watching me try to pedal through that impossible experience on stage in front of them. That was just one example of the utter humiliation endured during the nearly six-month whirlwind of learning as we prepared for our new career.

## Graduation

When graduation day finally arrived, I had achieved the rank of number six out of the thirty-seven candidates in my class. This ranking was compiled by averaging our academic, gun-range shooting and physical agility scores together. It was utterly shocking that I had elevated my status within this group from being nearly passed over due to my lack of physical abilities, to becoming sixth in rank after nearly six months, even though I had put forth many numerous hours of extra work. I was about to complete a lengthy, yet remarkable process of transformation. One day, six months earlier, I had been completely clueless regarding the law-enforcement field. Today I would become a commissioned peace officer for the State of Texas.

I was beaming with pride as my parents attended the ceremony, watching me up there wearing my Fort Worth Police uniform for the very first time. Both of them were clearly proud of me, too. I was so blessed that my Mom, Dad, and other family and friends were there to see me complete this first stage of the development of my identity as a police officer. I have definitely been privileged throughout the years to have parents who were, although sometimes surprised by my choices, behind me all the way in whatever I would strive to do in my life. Even though they voiced concern for my safety on this new job, I also believed that they had confidence in me. My Father has since passed away, but his approval, support, and love carried through in my heart over the years. My Mom continually shows confidence in me and support for me, which has always driven my efforts to endeavor even harder towards perfection in the law-enforcement field.

**Left:** *This photo was taken the first day of classes at the Fort Worth Police Academy. We all joked that this uniform, worn in class every day, made us look like a group of bus drivers!* **Right:** *This is my official academy graduation photo. You can tell that after months of intense physical training, I had trimmed myself down to the most physically fit I have ever been — and probably ever will be!*

*This photo was taken during the Class #85 academy graduation ceremony. Our former Chief, the late Thomas Windham, welcomed us to the force. This was one of the proudest moments of my life. I was blessed to have lots of family and friends there to usher me into my new career!*

# Chapter Five
## Out in the Field – *Left Field*

As I prepared for the first day of training out in the community, (which is considered "the field") with a veteran officer, I felt like the long lost fourth stooge. Because I came to this job fresh from my data-entry position in a mail-order pharmacy (and before that I was a clerk at a drug store) my only experience in the real world with criminal activity was with shoplifters. Imagine the level of ambivalence I harbored as I ventured out towards the streets for the first day. My feelings were not to be mistaken for *fear*. I was well trained and I felt extremely confident with my equipment, my knowledge of the law, policies and the competence of my fellow officers. I was not afraid. It was, instead, the feeling of being thrown into the deep end of the swimming pool – wearing a straight jacket (and I am not referring to our body armor, believe it or not) and this feeling engulfed me.

Today I would present myself for the first time as a Fort Worth Police officer. My reputation would begin. During my struggles to survive the probationary period it would quickly become apparent that nearly everything they taught us in the academy was "hypothetical." Things out in the world didn't really happen in a manner consistent with our training. Everything didn't fit into the context of one of those perfect little scenarios we practiced in the academy. Every situation was different, and potentially volatile. I felt overwhelmed, but I knew that everything would fall into place, as long as I reverted back to the intense training I had just completed. One thing I kept close in memory was a comment made by an academy instructor. "When an officer arrives on a scene, there is always at least one gun present." That meant every officer must focus on safety and observation in order to maintain control. If officers do not protect one another, those weapons could be compromised and everyone could be in more danger than they were before our arrival. With this thought on my mind as one of my primary tools for safety, I headed to work.

## FTO - First Training Officer

My duty assignment for the first month was evening shift. The hours for this watch were 2:15 p.m. to 10:30 p.m. I nervously drove up to the police sector located on the south side of town. I had never spent much time in this area, so I was uneasy because I did not know my way around the south side. I parked my blue, 5-speed, Mitsubishi Mirage in a spot in the far, back corner of the lot and hoped that I was not parking in some other officer's regular spot. I walked up to the door of the sector, and realized that I did not have access for entry into the door. There was a coded keypad style lock and I was clueless. I stood there, beginning to feel really out of place. A young officer dressed in a crisp, professional uniform finally approached the door and punched in the code for the keypad, while telling me the numbers. I was then led to the roll call room, where several officers were already sitting, filling out worksheets for the day. I sat in the chair that was closest to the back of the room. I was advised by one of the officers that I was sitting in someone's chair, and that I had better move. It was said in a joking manner, but it made me feel really stupid as I got up and moved over. Then I was told not to sit in the one next to it, either. I looked distraught, and the officer pointed out that any of the chairs in the first row were available. That was just great. Now I could sit up-front where everyone could stare at me. After playing musical chairs for a couple of minutes I was actually able to find a seat that didn't "belong" to a veteran officer. During roll call I could feel the beams of stares at the back of my head as I sat up front. I kept wondering if my hair was tied up properly, and if I looked okay, especially since everyone was looking at me. After all, I was the new kid on the block – the "rookie."

I was absolutely thrilled when my first roll call was over. I had been so self-conscious. Next was the introduction to my FTO (Field Training Officer). He looked like a nice enough guy. He was in his middle 30's, and he appeared to be less vicious than I had expected. Each of us academy graduates had been told to expect to work with "the devil himself" for the first three months while in training. My FTO was a veteran of about ten years. I could immediately sense that he was not thrilled to have a rookie to train. It is common knowledge to seasoned officers that if someone doesn't volunteer to train, but has a rookie assigned to them anyway, both the trainer and the trainee will be miserable for the duration of that arrangement. Later I would learn that my FTO was not happy to be training *in the least*. Basically, I was cutting into his hunting-magazine reading time by wanting to learn how to do my job. Unfortunately, I had been assigned to someone who was disgruntled about having to train me, in addition to being a "short-timer," who was dissatisfied with his career, and was looking for another job. Needless to say, I was rather distressed by the situation. My first several shifts turned into very long days, which stretched into a very long month of training on evening shift.

## Phase One: Evening Shift Training

In case you think I am exceptionally brave for writing so frankly about my first training officer, don't give me that much credit. He actually quit the Department and moved to another state about a year after I finished my training, (don't blame it on me – I was long gone to midnight shift, by then). As I indicated before, it was obvious that this man was in need of a career change. The mere act of sitting in the car with him for eight hours (or more) a day was excruciating to me. He made me nervous, and I was not getting the reinforcement I needed regarding work ethic, procedures, law, or anything of the sort, for that matter. As long as I parked under a shade tree in a grassy field on our beat and sat quietly as he read his hunting magazines, we got along just fine.

That is, until I started getting graded below standard for "self-initiated activity." Self-initiated activity is a mirror into the soul for a rookie officer. It indicates what type of work ethic the officer will adopt whenever they are "cut-loose" to work alone. This includes real beat-oriented police work, such as driving around the assigned beat-area between calls and checking the neighborhood for suspicious activity. It includes stopping traffic violators, speaking with pedestrians, or even watching a business, home or an entire area that has been recently targeted for criminal activity.

I was in need of some guidance in this area, since it was completely new to me. In my other jobs I could easily type letters from my boss, post rent payments, and even order cases of shampoo and hairspray to stock the shelf in my cosmetic department; but here - out here in the streets? In an area that was completely unfamiliar to me, I was supposed to just *go out and do something*. What could I do? I sat under a shade tree and waited for a call. When we got dispatched on something, I was elated. It was finally a chance to move around and do something! But after the call, you-know-who wanted to go right back to "the spot" and get back to reading. Then, at the end of the shift, we would go back to the roll-call room at the sector and review the days' trappings. This usually consisted of one or two calls for alarms or burglary reports, a lunch break, an assist of a stranded motorist, and a service-call to fill the cruiser up with fuel.

On the way back into the sector one evening, my training officer made an unsettling comment. He stated that I was not generating enough self-initiated activity and that I needed to drastically improve in that area, in order to avoid being graded progressively downward. I was livid. My reaction was probably surprising to him. I was truly astonished that he would even suggest such a thing, especially after making it clear to me that we were to be sitting in the field, under the shade tree all day, so he could proceed to read his magazines. I protested, and he told me that I needed to become more assertive and start my own routine. Well, great-guns and hallelujah! It was about time for him to finally let me do some police work!

Naturally this stimulated my adrenaline and I became preoccupied in my mind. We were headed into the driveway of the sector so he could fill out the daily report in my "rookie book." As I approached it the entrance, my subconscious kicked in. I reverted to auto-pilot mode, but I failed to remember which vehicle I was in. Instead of being in my personal five-speed Mitsubishi Mirage, I was, of course, in the automatic-transmission equipped patrol vehicle. My left foot pressed down on the clutch – oops! That was the brake! Everything in the car shifted to the front floorboard, including the numerous hunting and fishing magazines. If we had not been secured with our seatbelts, both my training officer and me would have flown through the windshield. I was mortified. We were sitting in the middle of the roadway, just prior to the driveway that led into the sector lot. It took me only a short time to realize what I had done, but my frazzled passenger was completely baffled. In addition to uncertainty about what had just happened, I detected a smidgen of anger. It was a pretty big smidgen, though. As a matter of fact, it was a significant enough smidgen that induced redness, and perspiration on my training officer's face. There were veins that were clearly visible popping out from his temple and forehead.

"What was that all about?" he yelled at me, as his eyes bugged out in disbelief.

"I am sorry, sir. I was preoccupied and I forgot that I was in the patrol car." I stuttered, "My subconscious kicked in and I thought I was in my personal car. I hit what I expected to be the clutch, but it was the brake."

He was not amused or even understanding about this little episode. He told me that I needed to be more careful, and that he was definitely marking me down for my driving skill in the book! I was so embarrassed that I wanted to offer to quit my job, if they didn't fire me, first! I knew I had to ride with this man for two more weeks, and he probably despised me and thought I was a real idiot by now.

Even though I left the sector that night embarrassed, I was still giddy, because I thought with two more weeks in this training phase, "I can at least start learning something tomorrow!" When I got to work the next day, however, for some strange reason my training officer wanted to drive. I didn't initially realize how badly I had traumatized him with my little mishap on the previous day. Although I didn't want to think about it again, I had to bring it up, because if I didn't, I would be imprisoned all day riding in the car with him. Knowing that he would be in control of everywhere we would go and everything we would do all day was a nightmare, and I wanted to be able to work on my self-initiated activity, as we had discussed. I figured a little more humiliation would be worth the trade-off for my freedom. I jumped into a rant, and as I spoke the words, I felt liberated.

"You know, yesterday when I accidentally slammed on the brakes, I did that because I am really nervous around you." I paused in awe of myself, because I had started something pretty difficult, and I had to finish it.

"How can I learn anything sitting in that field?"

"I just want to be a good officer, and I don't know how. I'm sorry for making a mistake. Please let me drive so that I can learn something."

I felt better, and it was easier for me to finish, "I am afraid that we need to just start all over, and try to do things differently for the next two weeks."

At this point, my partner pulled over to the side of the road, and switched places with me. He never said a word. He just got out, and switched with me, and off we went.

The next two weeks were much better, and for lack of a better way to initiate activity, I began to stop cars with burned-out headlights, after dark. If the driver had updated license and insurance, and was wearing a seatbelt, I would just give a warning to replace the lamp. If not, I would issue traffic citations for appropriate violations. This increased my productivity level, immensely, and I became more visible to the citizens in the neighborhood. Although this was not a desirable plan of action for a rookie in training, I knew that I had two more phases to go through. If I could make it through a month with my first FTO, surely the next two would be a piece of cake.

During the last two weeks, of course, my training officer just read his magazine while I wrote citations, *which beat sitting under the shade tree*. Overall, I didn't learn much during that entire phase of training. As a matter of fact, I learned more about what not to do, than how to be a good officer. I learned how to be more assertive, and in doing so, I had improved my communication skills. I learned how to conduct an extremely smooth and safe traffic stop. Ironically, the one call during evening shift training from which I learned the most occurred on a shift when my regular training officer was off sick. I had a substitute trainer for the day who volunteered our unit to work a shooting that came in late in the shift. I will detail that shooting, which was actually a suicide, in great depth later in this book.

## Phase Two – Day Shift Training

For my next phase, I went to the day shift, which was 6:15 a.m. to 2:30 p.m. My training officer was a corporal, which meant that he had been promoted from the rank of officer, and in doing so, was expected to train new officers. I didn't have to worry about where to sit during roll call, because he introduced himself to me and directed me to a seat next to him. I felt much better, already. This new FTO was very polite, interesting and pleasant to be around. He was a couple of years away from retirement. In spite of the traditional opinion that day-shift officers are ancient "dinosaurs" as they are often called, and that they are burned-out relics, I found the day-shift group was actually the opposite. The pace was slower, but they got the job done. There was calmness on the day shift which I had not seen on evenings. But much like evening shift, everyone was set in their ways, and had a routine. The difference, however, was that the day shift officers took the time to communicate with one another, and the camaraderie was so much more obvious. The beat meant something to these officers. They owned their beat. If a call went out, these officers jumped on it, and took care of it. They even knew the citizens with whom they were interacting. This was the real deal. These guys and gals on day shift knew how to work the South Side. Although it was truly contrary to everything I had expected, day shift was most instrumental in helping me to catch up. I was drastically behind regarding the level of knowledge and experience I should have accumulated in order to be in phase two. I didn't have to tell my new FTO about the first month. He read my "rookie book" and rolled his eyes with disapproval. He made it clear that his displeasure was not with me. It was the lack of documentation and explanation of experiences in my book. There was hardly any improvement, because there was hardly any activity. The lack of motivation that my prior phase FTO had exhibited irritated my new FTO. This guy was going to show me how to be a good police officer.

We had a daily routine, which gave me the feeling that we were partners. My new FTO would ask me questions like, "What would you do if...?" These scenarios kept me on my toes all day. This interaction with him built my confidence immensely and erased my feelings of inferiority. Each morning, after loading the vehicle and reviewing a few basic policies, we would drive through our beat, checking for abandoned stolen cars that had been dumped after a night of joy-riding by the local hoodlums and gangsters.

Often we would patrol our beat area, which was the industrial area just south of downtown, looking for evidence of overnight crime. We would actually often find the results of destruction at the hands of thieves who had worked during the immediately preceding darkness. These criminals would cut the wiring out of the air conditioning systems that were situated in the rear of doctor's offices and other business complexes. Sometimes we would arrive to the businesses and discover the ruins before the employees would. We would usually have much of the investigative information gathered, crime scene officers dispatched, photos taken, and evidence collected before the business owners would arrive. When they would finally arrive, we would inform them regretfully that they were in for an exceptionally hot day in the office because their cooling system had been destroyed. It was often heartbreaking to explain to them that this was due to a crook's need for $4.50 worth of wiring to sell so he could purchase his liquor for the day.

Unfortunately, scenes like this played out at least once a week. I remember thinking that if I were on the midnight shift, I could sit up somewhere on a roof and catch these guys. However, by the time we got out there for day shift, they were long gone, probably on their way from the scrap yard to the liquor store, just waiting for it to open.

After handling these crises for the local business owners, we would meet the officer who worked the beat next to us. He was my training officer's normal assist partner on most calls that required help. We would arrive at the local café called the "Paris Coffee Shop" for our daily routine. This place is legendary in Fort Worth for serving the most amazing food in the comfort of a close-community atmosphere. It is a famous icon in our City, where one will find regular customers present from all walks of life on any given day. Every morning I would order a scrumptious oatmeal muffin with hot chocolate and sit back in awe of the two veteran officers with whom I had the privilege of accompanying for breakfast. This was my favorite part of the day - sitting with these officers while being completely encompassed within the sensory bonanza of the café. I relished the sounds of clinking of cups and saucers, the aroma of coffee, bacon and muffins cooking in the kitchen, and the sight of smiling faces that greeted every new patron who entered the front door. It was great! I also pinched myself when I considered that I was part of an organization that had cultivated two such amazing characters as these guys were. They, too, were legendary, in every sense of the word. Even the dispatchers seemed to know to hold any calls for at least 15 minutes so that these two could finish their coffee.

Both officers gave me invaluable information on essential police-related issues. For instance, one fact they immediately made known to me was that the rookie buys the training officer's (and his friend's) breakfast, and a newspaper every morning. These guys were fun to be around, and made it easy for me to rethink the paradigm that field training officers were like Satan. I felt as if I was actually involved in the workday. After the daily coffee break, I remember sitting hidden in a shady spot behind a business where we could watch a bank and a shoe store on West Magnolia Avenue. My FTO wanted to be in a position where we could watch for criminals while he drilled me on my knowledge of the F.W.P.D. General Orders (policies), The Penal Code, Traffic Code, and our call signals. After doing that for awhile, we would drive the beat again, and he would teach me to identify houses and residents. He would ask me to take note of certain vehicles and remember which ones belonged and which were out of place. This guy had a real knack for training. It was a shame he would be retiring, soon, because he was an officer with integrity, knowledge, an incredible sense of humor, and compassion for everyone including citizens and other officers.

I learned and reinforced more information about police work in a day with him, than in a month with my first training officer, who was more concerned with hunting and sports magazines. Thank goodness for that, because my next assignment was going to be midnight shift. There wasn't much time to learn basics on "mids." We were going to be on the run from the minute we loaded up our gear and shut the cruiser door.

## Phase Three – Midnight Shift Training

Since my early childhood I had always harbored an overpowering desire to stay awake and seek out the mystifying secret world that was "overnight." I never wanted to go to sleep when I was little. When I did go to bed, I could hear sounds out in the world that made me yearn to be out there. I distinctly remember being in my room at night and staying awake as late as I could. I would hear big-rig trucks traveling down a nearby highway all through the night. I heard the shrill warnings of trains as they approached the nearby crossings. I could even hear the revving of hot-rod cars racing down the major thoroughfare that crossed the end of my street. I heard helicopters and airplanes fly over. I heard sirens from fire trucks, ambulances and police cars. I tried to imagine where all of these fast-moving, hustling and bustling sounds were ultimately leading to, and I desperately wanted to be out there to see what was going on. I know it probably makes no sense to most people, but I had a feeling that there was a secret world spinning all around me, and I was missing out on it. It made me angry and anxious inside. I felt a desperate desire to sneak out the window and creep to where the action was. This desire manifested itself deep in the pit of my stomach every night. As my parents turned out the light in my room and sent me "off to sleep" the feeling appeared, without fail, like a hungry dog at feeding time. I felt so imprisoned in my room, in my bed, at the age of nine and ten. My imagination led me through worlds of curiosity, excitement, and mystery that became an obsession to me. I accepted that there was an entirely different world out there after midnight (or even 10 p.m. - which was my bedtime). I anxiously awaited the day when I would be old enough to stay up all night, driving around following sirens and speeding cars. I was going to figure out what happens in that mysterious dark of night that was so far out of my reach. Each day simply became an opportunity for me to grow a day older, and a day closer to my freedom to explore the clandestine world of "the night."

The overnight shift in police work was definitely an awakening for someone like me who had been sheltered during her entire childhood. Nevertheless, it seemed that as I was working this shift, I was satisfying a deeply-rooted lifelong dream to be a part of the mysterious overnight existence. I could never explain the longing to simply be awake, aware and in the middle of whatever would happen in the deep darkness of the night. However, this feeling grabbed a hold of me, and took over a chunk of my soul for what would end up being three and a half years of my police career. Remembering those desperate nights in my room at night, feeling like the whole world was passing me by as I slept, I approached my third-shift training phase with an almost uncontainable enthusiasm.

Ultimately, I couldn't have been more fortunate. I was blessed, once again, with an officer who had a respectful attitude towards those of us who were in training. I was assigned to work with someone who had not yet promoted to the position of corporal, but who was completely qualified to instruct, guide and reinforce my learning during my final training phase. In spite of my indescribably amazing dayshift training officer and his flawless skills in the area of teaching, my midnight shift training officer quickly became my favorite trainer. He exhibited the pure dignity and respect that I, myself, longed to acquire. He made it clear that I was not inferior to him in any way, and that he was there to help me.

He wanted our month together to be a real partnership, and a mutual effort. He did not expect the world of me, but instead just the best that I could offer at this stage of my learning. With him as my guiding force, my best became more and more impressive. He told me something that I had not yet heard from a training officer. It changed my whole attitude, and boosted my confidence exponentially. He said, "When you are trained, you will be my partner out here on calls." He continued, "I want to make sure that you are comfortable enough in this job to cover me when we are out here dealing with God-knows-what in the middle of the night!"

He finished his statement with a genius thought. It made me wonder why more training officers did not feel this way: "What good would it do for me to make an enemy of someone who is going to be on my team in a few weeks?"

He was the first person to imply that I was actually going to become a successful police officer and a permanent member of this incredible family very soon. From that moment on, I have maintained utmost regard for him as a true, loyal friend and mentor. He is still with the Department, and has since travelled up the promotional ladder from officer, to corporal/detective, and will probably someday become a sergeant. Although we don't see one another anymore, I continue to hold a deep respect for him. That respect, which comes from knowing that I was treated with dignity by a trainer with integrity and compassion, will never fade.

As much as I learned from my dayshift-training officer (whom I must continue to assert was undoubtedly remarkable), my midnight training phase had just the right mix of activity, information recall, well-informed guidance and positive energy to be considered, by far, my most successful phase. All of the book learning, common sense and officer safety tips I had ever absorbed became shatterproof impressions in my mind during that one formative month. The confidence and real knowledge I was able to build through our "mutual partnership" would carry me through numerous life-threatening situations with confidence and competence. Years beyond that time it is still clear to me that I could never have been assigned to a better midnight shift training officer. This guy understood that even though I had a subconscious lifelong desire to be out on the midnight shift, it didn't mean that my body could just jump right into it without a struggle.

I will never forget the feeling of heaviness in every part of my body as I grew completely lethargic at around 4:00 a.m. every morning. It rivaled the times back in the academy when I tried to make that three-mile run with the class. For the first three weeks of this midnight-shift training I remember having to concentrate for a few seconds to make my left arm move towards the door handle on the car when I got out for our lunch break. It felt as if I had an anvil attached to my wrist. After eating "lunch" or whatever meal one has at 4:00 a.m. I was useless. I could hardly move to get back to the car. I rarely could even remember what I had eaten for my meal. I remember watching my training officer talking with fellow officers in the restaurant. I could see their lips moving, and I could hear a garbled exchange, but it was as if they were all speaking a foreign language that I did not comprehend. Everything was in slow-motion, and I felt almost intoxicated.

I was so completely wiped out from exhaustion that I could not remember one topic of conversation that had been discussed. I am sure that part of the exchange probably touched on the fact that I was staring ahead, blankly, with globs of grape jelly and biscuit crumbs sporadically perched upon my chin and shirt. Even so, no one made fun of me (at least not to my face). My training officer never belittled me for getting so tired, and I appreciated that. He understood the scope of my difficulties in learning to stay alert. He was a picture of empathy and compassion with regard to my dilemma, and I was so thankful to him. Consequently, every shift, for the first three weeks, we had a deal. He would have me drive for the first several hours, then, when I began to wilt, he would drive and take over the bulk of the actions necessary to complete our calls. Unless something really major happened, he would allow me to vegetate in the passenger seat. This usually happened after that lunch break, right after I dusted the crumbs and jelly off my chin. This was the slowest time of the shift, when time crept by and even most crooks and criminals were finally curled up somewhere in dreamland with their teddy bear. It was the hardest time to stay awake. Out of kindness, and maybe even a little bit of self-preservation, my training officer always took over the wheel for the remainder of the shift. He never made mention of this in my "rookie book."

One morning, during the third week or so of our month, we got a report of two vehicles racing one another in a residential neighborhood at about 4:30 a.m. When we arrived, we found two cars, still running, with doors hanging wide open at an intersection. It was clearly a case of two stolen vehicles left behind after a night of joy riding. Both had broken windows, popped trunks and busted steering columns. The suspects were long gone, but there was plenty of clean-up work for us to do at this location.

I was pretty lethargic, and I can still remember the feeling of impending doom that came over me when we drove up to the scene that morning. I knew there would have to be wreckers called, owners contacted, investigations completed and a report filed. I remember my training officer saying, "You know how to handle this call. What would you do?" I struggled to mumble the words that indicated protocol for this type situation. He agreed. He told me to sit in the car and wait for the wreckers. When they arrived, my job was to fill out the wrecker forms. He would take care of everything else, including the report. Wow! That was supposed to be my job as the rookie, and this guy was going to do it for me. He was amazing. I can still remember feeling the most dead-tired I have ever felt in my life that morning.

Changing shifts from evenings to days to midnight shift was very difficult on the body and mind. Unfortunately, my body and mind felt like dead weight. Even with my desire to be out there, to learn and prove myself, the duty hours dictated there would be a struggle for me to stay awake. I remembered back to the time when I was lying in my bed at the age of nine or ten, wishing I could be out there in the middle of whatever was going on. Now I'm thinking to myself, "I'm here and I see two abandoned, stolen cars. This should be exciting, but the thrill is gone. When's bedtime?" Thank God my partner knew I was struggling. He verified that I knew how to do my job, but he helped me to adjust to the new very difficult work hours. He achieved this with an unprecedented amount of patience and compassion. Thanks to him, I adjusted and eventually made the midnight shift my home for several years.

## Ghost Phase

After the two months on dayshift and midnight shift, respectfully, where I gained the most knowledge and confidence of all of my training, I had to go back to the evening shift and spend a final two weeks with my original training officer. This final phase is called the "ghost phase." This is because the training officer wears plain clothes and does not interact with citizens on calls. The activities of the entire shift are up to the probationary officer. In this phase, the decisions were going to be chosen and brought to fruition by me.

I could choose to stop a vehicle or not, write a citation or not, make an arrest or not, and every other option that was afforded to a shift of our work. During the two months since I had seen this training officer, my abilities had drastically improved, and I was prepared to work in the solo mode. I had to prove this to him, though. For two weeks, we perused the Southside for suspicious activity, answered calls for service, made routine traffic stops, and assisted other officers. I did all of this with no help whatsoever from my partner. As a result of my self-initiated activity, safe-handling of calls, and making sure my training officer got plenty of time to eat lunch, he gave me very good reports in my "rookie book." After my two-week ghost phase, my performance was evaluated by a sergeant, a lieutenant and ultimately a captain. Finally I was released to solo patrol. This was a turning point in my life. This was the day I was informed that I had assimilated well, performed well, and I was ready to protect and serve the City of Fort Worth as a real police officer.

I requested the midnight shift where I felt the most comfortable, and the request was granted. My childhood dream of being out in the world where I could know what occurred in the deep of the night was about to come true. I didn't yet realize that my childhood curiosities had been blissfully absent of details that were *better left unknown*. The things that go on after midnight involving police officers are rarely positive in nature. Even so, I was very excited because I would now be able to begin to cultivate my very own police identity and create my personal work ethic and reputation.

Over the course of my fifteen year career with the City I journeyed through several different assignments. After two years on midnight shift in patrol, almost two years on midnight shift in the Traffic Division assigned to the Driving While Intoxicated (D.W.I.) unit, two years in the Drug Abuse Resistance Education (D.A.R.E.) program, and nine years in the School Security Initiative (S.S.I.) unit, I feel as if I enjoyed a well-rounded career. During those fifteen years I cultivated an amazing amount of knowledge and experiences. I grew personally in numerous ways as a result of my exposure to these countless fascinating situations.

# My Full Body Armor

One thing I must relay is that this transition was not made without preparation in the form of my prayerful interaction with God. I asked for His guidance as I put on my uniform each day. I kept Him close to me as I walked into the roll call room, gathered my equipment, and entered the patrol vehicle. I whispered silent prayers as I rolled up to each call location, and every time I approached a vehicle for a traffic stop. I am quite confident that my prayers elicited a force field of protection around me on a regular basis, as will be evidenced through further reading of this book. As a matter of fact, I adopted a particularly relevant passage of scripture that I would apply to my daily life as an officer whose job it was to protect and serve those around me. Just as the soldier prepares for physical warfare, I tried to prepare for that, as well as for the spiritual warfare I would certainly encounter. Although symbolic in nature, this passage represented comfort and assurance for me, each day.

The imagery in Ephesians 6:12-18 elicited confidence for me each day as I proceeded through my days, praying for God's provision and protection:

12*For we wrestle not against flesh and blood, but against principalities, against powers, against the rulers of the darkness of this world, against spiritual wickedness in high places. 13Wherefore take unto you the whole armor of God, that ye may be able to withstand in the evil day, and having done all, to stand. 14Stand therefore, having your loins girt about with truth, and having on the breastplate of righteousness; 15And your feet shod with the preparation of the gospel of peace; 16Above all, taking the shield of faith, wherewith ye shall be able to quench all the fiery darts of the wicked. 17And take the helmet of salvation, and the sword of the Spirit, which is the word of God: 18Praying always with all prayer and supplication in the Spirit, and watching thereunto with all perseverance and supplication for all saints; 19And for me, that utterance may be given unto me, that I may open my mouth boldly, to make known the mystery of the gospel; (KJV)*

For current officers, this passage affords a great sense of comfort through the practice of meditation each day before heading to work. Future officers preparing for a career in law-enforcement would also be wise to cultivate a relationship with Jesus Christ, and with God's Word. This practice will undoubtedly provide necessary peace that cannot be found elsewhere. Believe me when I say that in the course of this career, peace will routinely escape as a result of the sometimes wretched circumstances experienced. The only way this elusive peace can possibly be restored is through that relationship with Christ and with knowledge of the comforting Scriptures.

# Chapter Six
## The Horrors of Mental Illness

*"For my enemies are whispering against me. They are plotting together to kill me. They say, "God has abandoned him. Let's go and get him, for there is no one to help him now." (Psalm 71:10-11 NLT)*

Mental illness is a prevalent issue in society today, and its presence must not be overlooked. Some truly remarkable experiences fill the daily lives of the mentally ill citizens with whom we share our City. I have considered it a privilege to encounter the wide array of personalities I have experienced during my tour with the Fort Worth Police Department. Regarding my interactions with citizens, whether the problem stems from bad decision-making, bad luck or from a devastating mental illness doesn't really matter. What does matter is learning empathy, compassion and genuine ways to help them. This has always been my underlying goal, and undoubtedly played a part in my eventual segue from the law-enforcement field into counseling. Unfortunately during the first occasions I dealt with these types of issues I did not yet have an adequate amount of proper education and insight into the horrors of mental disorders.

In this section I will touch briefly upon a phenomenon perpetuated by mental instability that renders the reporting citizen functional, yet almost constantly disturbed by a form of paranoia. My purpose for doing this is to show the differing facets of reality with which officers must become acquainted in the course of a "normal" day. These people harbor a unique view of life. They often regularly experience delusions of persecution and continually harbor ideas of reference (thinking that everything in the world complements a conspiracy involving them). These delusions lead them to believe that the world is full of secret units, spies, aliens, and others who would bring doom and gloom to our society (or our entire planet). As a result of my interest in the fields of counseling and psychology, these people have always fascinated me. One truth that must be noted is this: just as in other stressful situations officers must encounter, sometimes the mechanism of humor is used as a self-preservation technique when dealing with confusing and unusual circumstances. Again, I must emphasize that there is no intention of disrespect to the citizens highlighted in the following accounts.

While I have never found anything in the Scriptures that categorically prohibits the possibility of other life in our universe, I have also never actually been able to catch even a fleeting glimpse of an alien from outer space. Even so, there are those who believe in "life on other planets" on some level. Those who hold this belief do so both fervently and with vivid imagination about its existence.

A certain type of mysterious occurrence I missed when I was a small child listening to the sounds of the night was of the alien warfare that obviously took place on our rooftops. It is an experience that only certain people have been privileged to behold. In this City, the event rears its violent nature during the deep, mystic, dark hours of the night. It is the *"aliens shooting through the roof"* phenomenon. I can remember more than a few individuals who reported just such activity to me on a regular basis (and many of them seemed to live in my beat area district).

Consequently, as a result of my lack of in-depth professional training at the time with regards to ways of effectively assisting those who experienced such delusions, I did what any good beat officer would do. I became well acquainted with these folks in order to build up a rapport, and then I taught myself a few highly technical ways to ward off the attacks. When I was summonsed to these investigations, I had the background knowledge, the tools, and the tricks up my sleeve to send those conspiring, bothersome aliens back to their home planet. Because of my deficit in training regarding the sensitive field of mental illness at the time, most of my tools and tricks boiled down to some type of creative manipulation involving aluminum foil.

# Marge

One particular morning at a regular call location, upon my arrival I was hurried into the home and the door was shut swiftly behind me.

"Quickly," she said, "They'll get us." As I surveyed the room I observed foil sculptures and television antennas strategically placed throughout.

"They are shooting at me again tonight," the lady I'll call "Marge" whispered, quietly, as she held up a sheer, plastic light fixture sheet, designed to cover a fluorescent light. The plastic was covered with foil and she was holding it over her head.

"I can deflect them with this," she continued, "but they are hitting pretty hard and it's beginning to penetrate my shield." Marge showed me the holes in the foil where the sharp plastic had ripped through.

"You've got to do something." She pleads, "It is only getting worse."

Through time and experience I learned that the only successful course of action where Marge was concerned involved *more foil*. I quickly realized that I didn't even need to go to the kitchen. Marge had a rather hearty supply in a crate, sitting right there on the sofa. I grabbed a roll and began wrapping it around her shield of plastic.

"Let me fix it for you." I said, "I'll give it a double layer that they can't penetrate!" After about three minutes of wrapping foil, tucking the corners tightly and testing it out on myself, the new and improved alien laser dart shield was ready for business. I assured Marge that she was all set for the night. We placed the shield underneath her comforter on her bed, and she felt much better, ready to try to get some sleep. I also tried to comfort her by telling her that I had stationed the S.W.A.T. team on her neighbors' rooftops to capture any aliens that were determined enough to come back and shoot at her again. She was somewhat content, at least for the time being.

The scary part of this story is that Marge suffered from sleep deprivation because of her adamant beliefs regarding her delusions. During the night she hardly ever slept. What was her livelihood? During the day she ran a daycare center out of her home. She told me that she cared for up to eight small children every week-day. Apparently, during the day, she was able to function without revealing any adverse effects from her mental illness. Even so, I often wondered how she could present herself as being perfectly healthy during the daytime (in the name of her livelihood), but would always transform into such a miserably disturbed individual by nightfall.

## Weldon

Next is one of my favorite people who I regularly encountered. I enjoyed visiting with him because he intrigued me so much with his imagination. Besides that, he loved to write out his thoughts in the form of letters to the police, to document any possible future foul play.

I'll call this guy Weldon. Fortunately Weldon did not run a daycare center. He did, however, like to eat at a fast food burger restaurant on W. Berry Street close to a large local university. As with most of those who fear governmental conspiracies, he didn't sleep much, so he would frequent this location around 4:00 a.m. Incidentally, this was one of the only places open in the early hours of the morning in my district. So when I went for my lunch break, I would run into my buddy Weldon more often than not. He regularly had those handwritten notes detailing his latest crisis concerning his very own conspiracy theories. He would always deliver those notes to me, along with a request that I notify the homicide division in case the government agents ever succeeded in killing him. I have included some excerpts of writing from Weldon's notes, so that you can understand the intensity of his despair:

*"Dear Officer:*
*I found this broken glass on the floor of my bedroom at (omitted address). I have broken no glass recently. A government compensated person must have left this broken glass on the floor of my bedroom. Previously I cut my foot badly because of broken glass that was left on the floor of my carpeted bedroom. I suppose the criminals who harass me also steal my inventions, research experiments, and product design. No one has paid me for the product design, process design, or inventions that the industrial spies stole. My carpet is brown so broken glass is hard to see. I'm not breaking any laws as far as I know. The investigators who investigate me and persecute and harass me are the crooks. They stole more than one dozen new fuel formulas from me, while they torture me with transmitter applied neuro-stimulation of my brain. Their long term conduct has caused several deaths*

and they're not changing a policy of assaulting people with electric shocks. It's capital murder. They cause people to have symptoms of mental illness as a result of remote control applied neuro-stimulation. Those people think they're untouchable."

"Dear Officer:
My sister gave me half of a pizza at about 8-10 p.m. Friday. I started feeling really intoxicated and bought a cup of coffee. I was strongly intoxicated on some type of sedative/tranquilizer/painkiller type drug at that time. I realized that there was dope on the pizza I just ate or there was dope in the coffee I drank with the pizza or they shot me with another drug dart or the electronic implant in my head was altering my brain function by remote control electric stimulation of my brain. It felt like a potent narcotic which wears off in about four hours or more. I am being used in drugging experiments that I did not volunteer for. I have not been paid for them using me either."

"Dear Officer:
The organized young crooks working off of the university campus seemed to have sent a stupid young man to sit at my table while five or six of his buddies were in the dining room at (fast food restaurant). I go there to be around other people without spending a lot of money AND a pretty, smart, slim, educated woman might decide I'm irresistible while I'm there.
I've seen the university crowd send one young man to start a fight with me while twenty of his buddies were nearby. I've seen six university men beat one man so bad that an ambulance took him to the hospital. I don't know if this occurrence with the obituaries is only psychological warfare, or if it's a real serious death threat. If they are convicted, they could get the death penalty AND I'm blowing the whistle on their research group.
Those university young men don't seem to respect me."

As you can see, Weldon definitely suffered from a mental illness. The symptoms he exhibited seemed to point to paranoid personality disorder. In this disorder, the sufferer experiences delusions of persecution and harbors a constant suspicion and mistrust of others. Fittingly, he was certain that he was the subject of a super-secret governmental conspiracy and a related dangerous experiment that somehow consisted of an implanted chip and neuro-transmitters. One night he detailed how government agents posing as college students put something in his drink at the restaurant in order to jam his brain waves. He said they were all taunting him.

"See, look over there." A group of students were having a meal after a late night out, and happened to be donning university colors, much to Weldon's dismay.

"They are all wearing those purple shirts. Those are to intimidate me." He said.

Another time, while he was running errands, he reported that the agents had moved things around in his home while he was gone, just to see if he would notice. Poor Weldon was always on the run trying to find ways to secure his home better so that no one could get in and conduct those unauthorized, yet systematic experiments on him. One day he went to a local hardware store to buy a yardstick and a deadbolt lock. On that particular visit he was convinced that the cashier had used the bar-code scanner on the cash register to activate vertigo and dizzy spells through his microchip implant.

"It caused sharp pains in my stomach," He said, "and I got dizzy. I know it was the secret laser beams in the bar code reader!"

Weldon was miserable as a result of his paranoia and delusions. On several occasions I would try to discuss his mental health issues with him from the standpoint of directing him to help. He had been evaluated by psychological professionals, and did not want any further contact with mental health providers. His behavior was not endangering to himself, so I had no further options other than to attempt to comfort him.

Consequently, I tried to persuade him that the secret agents had deactivated his microchip and that they were no longer interested in him as a specimen. Weldon wasn't buying it, and unfortunately he never quit looking over his shoulder, even up until the time I was transferred from his district to another assignment.

## Stanley

It is sometimes difficult to ascertain whether or not an individual is truly in distress, or if he is simply seeking attention from first responders.

However, in the case of this young man who I will call Stanley, there was no doubt. Stanley was unquestionably experiencing delusional thoughts. His suicide attempt led to his being admitted into the hospital for evaluation. Stanley had taken his parents' car out and intentionally wrecked it. Before being taken into custody for his safety, he provided this letter:

*"Sorry for looking bad. I thought it was my destiny to prove how good America is, so I wanted to take my life tonight, doing this to show a smart American died for the fear of Jack the Ripper. I got all upset at the UK a long time ago for whining about how bad America is. But tonight I just showed the world "don't try this at home."*

*I slowed down in time to save my life, because Hawaii is where I am going.*

*My parents are \*\*\*holes so I am moving to Hawaii next June to get away from home. To my fellow Americans that thought trying to prove America is awesome, I ask nicely for this offer: Please start a charity to help me move away from home before June. Mom and dad I brought the car into this to upset you both for all of the BS you have been throwing in my face. I want a job also. I was fired over nothing!"*

Once again, it becomes clear that the human imagination can run wild, and unfortunately, the related human body has to go along for the ride. Thankfully Stanley did receive a mental health evaluation at the hospital that night, and his intentional car crash did not harm anyone other than himself.

## Raymond

Occasionally I would have a family member or friend come out and ride along with me on a shift. It was always fun to watch reactions of those who were not accustomed to some of the things that happen out in the world, especially on midnight shift. From time to time I would encounter people out in the field who, like Mary and Weldon, believed that someone or some thing was after them. Such paranoia would drive these people to act in the most mysterious ways. One night, when I had my cousin riding with me, we encountered just such an individual. I will call him Raymond.

Travelling down I-35, we encountered Raymond walking in the center median of the freeway. After pulling up on the opposite side of the roadway, I exited the vehicle and approached him. He was acting very nervous and I could tell that he was in need of some assistance. He was in serious danger. He believed that someone was after him, and was acting very irrationally. His situation was imminent because he was literally out in the middle of the freeway, hallucinating.

I, too, became uneasy, realizing that if Raymond took one step in the wrong direction, he would be in the traffic lane with speeding cars. He did not know me or trust me, so I had to be very careful to move slowly and speak clearly to him. This was very scary for me, because a mistake in judgment on my part could potentially have caused a tragic outcome.

Another unit made the scene with me, and after several moments of conferring with Raymond gingerly we were able to talk him into coming off of the freeway. We helped him climb over the concrete median and I placed him in the back of my car. All the time, my cousin was watching from the front passenger seat of my patrol vehicle.

After I placed Raymond in my car, I shut the door and remained outside for a few moments talking to my assist officer about my plans to take Raymond to John Peter Smith Hospital. I did not realize that I had left the window open in the cage that divided the front of the passenger compartment from the back. Consequently, Raymond leaned up into the window opening and began a conversation with my cousin. During that time, he asked her if we were going to hurt him. She explained that we were only trying to help him. He was not convinced. He continued to ask her questions, to which she did not have the answers. This made her extremely uneasy, as she was not prepared to be left alone with a delusional subject in the car, much less have a conversation with him answering his concerns about my intentions.

When I got back in the car she indicated to me that he had leaned through the window and had been asking her all kinds of questions. She was not particularly happy about this. Understandably, Raymond made her nervous, and she did not know what to say to him. When we arrived at the hospital, I had to exit the vehicle again to take care of the details of getting Raymond checked in to the hospital. I was standing right outside the door, but I later found that I was still not close enough, in my cousin's opinion. While I was out of the car, Raymond asked her if I was going to take him into the hospital. She replied, "Yes, she is going to take you in there to get you some help. You need some help tonight."

Raymond replied to her, "No. Please don't let her take me in there. This is an evil place. They are going to barbecue me in there! This place barbecues people right inside there."

My cousin did not have any idea how to counter that concept. As a result, she just continued to reassure him that he was not scheduled to be the main course for the hospital menu, but rather that he was going to be evaluated and provided with some help for his hallucinations.

Eventually I returned to the car and helped Raymond into the hospital for the professional assistance he required. He went reluctantly. When I finished and returned to the car where my cousin was waiting, she let me have it! She let me know that she had felt extremely uncomfortable being left alone with Raymond. His strange behavior was something I had dealt with before on many occasions. For my cousin, however, it was a different story. The events of that night happened over thirteen years ago, and she still does not let me forget about it. She always tells others how I left her alone in the car with a delusional man who stuck his head through the window, invading her personal space. That ride-along experience was one that definitely made a lasting impression on her, and probably for some not-so-good reasons.

## Angie

My fifth story details the life of a lady I'll call Angie. Angie was an older lady who lived alone, near an industrial area and a set of train tracks. Angie was very well known in the area as being rather boisterous and unique. She would regularly paint her home and her fence different, bright colors with messages to passers-by. She was not in my patrol district, but she lived on the border of it, and often times I would drive by and see her out on her roof, watching for the secret agents and aliens.

This lady was vigilant. She would actually sit on her roof. I guess she figured if she was up there she could head them off! Unfortunately, her vigilance came with a price to many of those innocent passers-by. Angie believed some vehicles in the passing traffic contained alien or government spies, who were sent to spy on her because she knew about the secret alien / government project. She believed that the industrial warehouse behind her house was creating nuclear weapons for the aliens to use against those of us here on earth. When the trains would go by, she reported that government agents would sneak onto the train and try to assist the aliens who were making bombs at the warehouse in their escape. When some cars would pass by her house, she would often throw things at them, ranging from rocks to sticks to oranges. Whatever she had up on that roof, it became a projectile weapon against the alien conspiracy. I was a bit thankful that she was not in my district, not because I didn't want to help her, but rather because I didn't have my own foil covered shield to fight off her citrus ammo!

Angie became legendary in our city, and unfortunately, the local university students learned of her theories and eccentric ways. She became a bit of a tourist attraction for them. They would drive by on a regular basis and taunt the poor lady. Eventually her reputation earned her an infamous status in her community. No matter what, though, Angie would be out there on top of her roof giving the aliens, the government agents and the alleged spies a ration of trouble they never expected. She was a tough lady, and nothing seemed to discourage her from standing up for herself, especially when she had a nice, ripe bag of oranges up there with her!

# Chapter Seven
## The "Oldest Profession"
*[This chapter contains sexual content, drug use and undesirable language]*

The next fascinating task that took me into a realm of the unknown in my new career was the assignment to work as a prostitute during a decoy-sting operation. The vice unit worked these details in conjunction with patrol a few times during my assignment on midnight shift. They would move through different areas (beats) throughout the city and use different officers as "fresh faces" to generate the appearance that we were participants in the numerous illegal sex crimes which plague our area. Although prostitution is a despicable crime, this endeavor definitely fits in the category that cultivates humor.

### It's All in the Details

Excessive occurrences of sex-for-sale crimes are devastating to the community because of resulting disease, drug use, alcoholism and violence. Even in light of the seriousness of this plight, the idea of me being out on the streets acting like I knew what I was doing was a joke. We did the bulk of these prostitution sting "details" within six months after I graduated from the police academy. I still knew almost nothing about the real world and life on the streets. Believe it or not, though, we were always successful despite my ignorance.

I was often accompanied by another female decoy officer, several backup vice officers and supervisors with radio contact, and a troop of patrol unit "chase cars" on standby in the nearby neighborhood. After being approached by the potential "customer," it was our duty to indicate the type of vehicle, license plate, description of the driver and finally, the sex-for-hire deal that was made, including the monetary amount that was agreed upon. This was accomplished through the presence of a clandestine body microphone that was tucked inside of our clothing and taped to the chest. For me, it was placed just underneath my tank top. Wearing this type of device always made me feel nervous. I continually obsessed that my normal movements might somehow loosen its grip from my skin, rendering it visible, thereby blowing my cover.

Sometimes, however, we did these details without the assistance of the vice unit. During these times the body microphones were not used. There would always be a backup officer nearby who appeared to be a member of the community. These guys blended in as drunks, homeless people, or drug dealers. While the backup officer strategically blended in with the surroundings, he had a radio tucked underneath his jacket that was used to relay the descriptions and the details of the attempted transactions, and a pistol hidden away that was ready for business should the need arise.

On different occasions we generated as many as nineteen, twenty-one and twenty-three arrests, over the course of two or three hours. Arrests were usually actually handled in the form of citations which would summon suspects to court after they propositioned one of the decoy officers regarding a sex act for money (or other means of payment). That is, unless they happened to be occupying a city vehicle, which unfortunately, happened on at least one occasion. In one particular instance I remember, the poor guy (yes – a criminal who made a bad decision but who got a much worse consequence than others because he did so on city time in a city vehicle) was taken into custody, booked in, and his vehicle was towed as his supervisor was contacted. Actually, we were accosted on several occasions by owners or employees of prominent local businesses, as well as by delivery drivers from well-known consumer product companies who would stop in their marked delivery vans!

Surprisingly, on one particularly successful evening in the summertime, we generated thirty-seven arrests in just over two hours. That detail was one of the first ones I ever participated in with the Vice Unit, actually. In order to set up for this detail, I had to bring some special clothing to work with me. This consisted of stone-washed light blue denim cut-offs that were too short, and a black tank top that was also too short, and some old, worn out sneakers. I intentionally neglected to wash my hair or to put makeup on so that I could look a little bit more "rough" than normal that night (not that anyone noticed). I put my hair up in a ponytail and grabbed a lighter and couple of cigarettes from my buddy who smoked. He was going to be my close-cover backup officer for the evening. This officer, who is now deceased, was quite a character, actually. He always added an unforgettable facet of entertainment to our endeavors. He arrived for duty dressed like he came straight from the streets. He was not in the least afraid to yell expletives to the other drug dealers and prostitutes in the area, cautioning them that we were "working this corner tonight," and they needed to move on out of the area. We often wondered if he was able to assimilate *a bit too easily* to that lifestyle. Of course, he had plenty of real-life examples on a nightly basis to inspire him, and as a result he did a fantastic job of protecting me by blending perfectly into the environment.

To further enhance his credibility factor, my backup officer acquired an empty forty-ounce Schlitz Malt Liquor beer bottle and went to the 7-Eleven. At the soda-fountain he filled the glass bottle up partially with some dark soda, and the rest of the way with clear soda. This netted the perfect appearance of the amber colored beer that had once filled the bottle. He was able to drink on duty, now! He perched himself awkwardly upon the nearby wall at the intersection of Hemphill Street and West Jefferson Avenue (near Allen Avenue), which happened to be one of the more prevalent drug, alcohol and prostitution headquarters for the South side of Fort Worth. He acted like he was drunk, just lingering halfway between passing out and observing the events of the night. Despite his appearance, he was extremely alert and ready for business. The locals knew we were the police, and this aggravated them quite a bit. However, the potential customers did not know, and they were our target during these types of details.

Some of the characters that patronize the sex-for-hire market on the streets seemed to have some rather disturbing ideas about what should constitute acceptable payment for such services. Many of these propositions can now be looked upon with humor, but they actually proved to be utterly insulting at the time. For instance, here are some of the actual payments offered to me in return for sex acts on different occasions:

- $1.25 and six pack of beer;
- $7.17 (because that is all of the loose change that was in the cup holder of the truck);
- A value meal from Whataburger and a forty ounce bottle of beer;
- $5 and a freshly rolled marijuana cigarette;
- One man (disturbingly enough, accompanied by his wife) offered the generous payment of allowing me to sleep at their home for the night after I completed my duties there;

I always reported those deals over my hidden microphone with a combination of satisfaction (that such insulting individuals were about to be issued a very expensive citation), displeasure (with the idea that these people actually thought I would perform sex acts for such menial wages) and sorrow (that some of the people on the streets might just accept such an offer on a regular basis). When those deals were made, I secretly hoped that when the officers in the "chase vehicle" stopped them, they would somehow get an extra citation for a traffic violation, or become arrested for being intoxicated or possessing drugs, as did occasionally happen. It wasn't personal, but some of those people had an inordinate amount of disrespect for humanity on the simplest level, and I wanted them to pay!

One aspect of these details that was skillfully anticipated by the police and yet customarily disregarded by the actual prostitutes is the high risk of danger. The possibility of the unknown is very real for any individual who approaches vehicles to speak with complete strangers. It amazes me that the established regular prostitutes would develop the habit and ability to approach these vehicles with a complete absence of concern for personal safety. This is just another testament of the desperation that accompanies drug and alcohol addiction for many.

The recognition of possible danger was accompanied by caution and for me, sometimes sheer terror. I remember standing near the light pole at my intersection, holding a cigarette and acting like I was smoking as I would walk up to the passenger window of the numerous vehicles that would stop. The drivers, often in nervous and hasty voices would say, "Hop in!"

I would reply, "No. not here. There are too many cops around here. What do you want?" The customer would then often ask me, "Are you a cop?" This was answered with an adamant "*Expletive* No! I am not a cop! I am so sick of them jacking me up! That's why you gotta pull over here out of the street or they'll nab you!" My apparent displeasure with the police seemed to throw them off guard and garnered a bit of credibility for me, as well. Usually, by this time, the driver would pull over onto the side street. Here, I could usually spend a bit more time securing the deal.

Afterwards, I would always say, "Hey, pull down there to Lipscomb Street. It is about two blocks down. The cops are too stupid to hang down there; I'll run down there to get in so we don't get caught." To this, the customer often breathed a sigh of relief and gunned it for Lipscomb Street. This was how it normally went.

Before I move on, I will make a guilty confession. Being able to lose my inhibitions out there by acting like I had no decent upbringing, cursing excessively, and talking with no regard for common decency was actually very entertaining for me. I felt like an actor auditioning for a role each time a potential "customer" would pull up to me on the street. Actually, I guess I was a pretty good actor, since I repeatedly sent folks down to Lipscomb Street to get their tickets by convincing them that I wasn't a police officer.

The scariest part of the whole situation was how much I enjoyed acting like a criminal. As I stood there waiting for the next vehicle, I thought to myself, "How can I be getting paid to do this, especially considering that the prostitutes out here get paid to really do that?"

However, there were those occasions where the driver became angry, spooked, and just plain scary. I had one guy say, "Just get in the *expletive* truck so we can go." I refused, and he sped away, furiously. That is precisely the type of guy I felt we needed to catch, but who always seemed too guarded to become caught up in our operation. Although the venture of working these prostitution details was exciting for me as a rookie officer, it was definitely no game. The danger was real, the risks were overwhelming, and the impact of these street crimes are still ultimately staggering to the surrounding communities.

*It was near this historic Fort Worth motel in the 1700 block of Hemphill Street that many of our prostitution details took place. I stood by this intersection in the dark of night, waiting for the next potential "customer." My cover officer would perch himself nearby on this wall and act like a drunken transient.*

## Carley

Almost all street-level officers have an exclusive opportunity to cultivate relationships with the citizens on the beat area they patrol. This even includes the fascinating individuals who thrive upon illegal street life. It is not impossible to treat those people with respect. The letter of the law drives some officers to use up an entire citation book in a week on the same individuals, whereas the spirit of the law dictates that ever so often, it might be a good idea to spend some time getting to know these people, instead of causing them a hassle. This is true, especially if you work the same area regularly.

Making acquaintances and developing rapport with those who are labeled "undesirable" is actually a very smart endeavor that benefits the officer. It shows respect for the citizen, it develops a sense of trust, and it develops an informative relationship that can be used when needed to gather reliable information. It makes the officer human in the eyes of the citizens. If a life or death situation should occur, this person could be our only hope for life-saving assistance. Personally, I would much rather have these people on my side, than not. I would hate to be shot, laying in the road, and have the prostitute that I just wrote twelve citations to simply stand by and watch as I bleed to death.

Even more importantly, treating these people with respect models Christian behavior. Acts of mercy, compassion, and respect for those less fortunate are perfect ingredients in the recipe for Christ-like behavior. Who is going to show them a way out of that sinful and destructive lifestyle if those who know better don't take the opportunity to do so?

*"…Look around you! Vast fields are ripening all around us and are ready now for the harvest…the fruit they harvest is people brought to eternal life." (John 4:35-36 NLT)*

As this scripture implies, the mere position of working as a patrol officer out in the midst of the world is an opportunity to show the love of Christ to lost souls. Jesus Himself chronicles his time of interaction with those who appear to be the least desirable in cultural terms. As a result, it is my belief that in the context of "protecting and serving," these citizens, too, deserve our respect. Our contact with them may be the only time they ever receive interaction with someone who genuinely cares about them.

As a result of my philosophy in this regard, I actually became amiable with a few of the regular prostitutes who used to work the area around Hemphill Street and Allen Avenue. At times I would see them sitting at a bus stop, or walking towards the nearby convenience store and would approach them just to check on them. They knew me, and they knew I was not there to hassle them. I was truly interested in them and in their well-being. Maybe that comes from my being a female; maybe it comes from my being a Christian. I am not really sure, but I always felt a desire to try to find a tangible way to help remove them from that lifestyle. I would often sit silently in my car praying for these women, asking that something would convict their hearts before they were killed one way or another from the dangerous activity they carried out, daily. Even so, all the compassion, care and assistance in the world would not help those who did not want to change. It would have to be left up to divine intervention, and that is where most of these women would remain - standing somewhere in the middle, between the worldly realm of reality and the forthcoming conviction of God.

I did develop a particularly interesting relationship with one young prostitute and drug addict who I will call Carley. At the time, she was an incredibly beautiful young lady, about twenty, who had come from an affluent home. She had been a cheerleader in high school in a very nearby suburb. She was estranged from her parents, but when she would have a charge filed against her she would call them. They never failed to immediately send the money needed to bail her out. It was rather unfortunate because their enabling of her behavior drove her deeper and deeper into a cesspool of drugs, alcohol, unprotected sex, disease, and violence. I cannot tell you how many times she was beaten by her "boyfriend" who was also her pimp. I would see her regularly in the neighborhood with either a busted lip or a black eye in healing stages. Sometimes I would see her limping from bruises on her legs.

Occasionally I would catch her in a slump, when she did not have the money for drugs, and was sober for the moment. She was agitated, fidgety, but without prospective customers at 3:00 a.m. on a Tuesday morning, she would take the time to talk openly with me about personal issues. That is what fueled my compassion for her. She was honest. I can overlook a lot of despicable and condemning behavior in someone, especially if that person can be honest with me – and she always was.

We would exact an ethical (and legal) trade-off that benefitted both of us. I would trade a trip to the convenience store to get a snack and a coffee in exchange for her spending the time to answer some of my questions. She would tell me about the lifestyle implications of being a drug user and a prostitute. She would divulge details of some of her quests with customers. One time I asked her to tell me about her most unusual encounter with a "client." She happily relayed to me the details of a regular customer who would always pay her $200 to participate in a sex-act which involved a plastic nasal-spray bottle while he watched her (I will not further elaborate on the details of this endeavor. It will be better that way - believe me)! She seemed proud of this regular customer, because he would pay her so well, and she did not even have to touch him.

"Jackpot!" She exclaimed proudly when recollecting him.

"He should be around in a couple of days," she reflected with anticipation.

"$200 buys a lot of *expletive* (drugs)."

## Pins And Needles

We were on a roll, and Carley was enjoying my reaction to her stories. As a result, she shared with me an extensive list of her prostitution memoirs. Those chronicles alone could fill a very interesting, yet not very wholesome book. I will not elaborate on details, because they are obviously in very poor taste. The things she detailed were sometimes so disgusting that I asked her, "How can you do that?" or "How can you even be in the room while that is happening?" Carley's answer was, "They are paying me."

When I asked her those questions, I was trying to diminish the imagery of a certain regular customer she had just told me about. This man had a sexual fetish that involved inflicting pain to his male anatomy during sexual stimulation. He would pay Carley to provide service to him while he fastened his skin together in some very sensitive areas with safety pins. This made me cringe.

Carley laughed, "He is the one paying me," she said, in a nonchalant manner, "That is how I get hooked up (with drugs), so whatever it takes."

"That's what he likes – it works out for both of us – a few pins for him and a few needles for me!"

## Yo-Yo Effect

As well as I knew Carley, I wasn't really surprised at what she would do for money. Sadly, her entire life revolved around using drugs and that seemed to be her sole purpose for being alive. On the other hand, however, I was surprised at what others *would ask her to do* for money. That thought, most certainly, is very disturbing.

Carley would tell me of drug and liquor binges in dingy cockroach infested motel rooms. She describe being so numb with intoxicating drugs that she could remember only what seemed like fuzzy slow-motion details of where she had been for days at time. She did not seem to mind at all that she had lost a day here and there to a stupefied state of intoxication. She insisted that her need for crack or methamphetamine was so intense that she would do anything for it. She did not care about her life. All she cared about was getting her next hit of meth or crack. She was being brutally honest.

During the span of my career Carley did at least three stints in prison for drug possession. She would go into the system very slender, almost gaunt from her lifestyle of drug and alcohol binges and barely eating any food. She would come out weighing about two-hundred extra pounds. Unfortunately, her institutional weight gain simply perpetuated her desire to regress to the same lifestyle upon her release. As a result, she would shed the weight again within weeks, perpetuating a yo-yo effect on her body. This relapse was expected, actually, because she always told me that her goal in life was to be high whenever possible. Prison cut into her drug-use time. Ultimately, her singular goal in getting out of prison was to gain access to the hard drugs she had been separated from while incarcerated.

Carley still resides on the Southside of Fort Worth, and is miraculously still alive. I have not seen her or heard from her in several years, but the beat officers who work the area encounter her from time to time. I still pray for her. I believe she will eventually become tired of that lifestyle, if her body does not give out on her, first.

## Birth Out Of Control

The next woman, who I will call Lee Ann, was another regular prostitute who worked the area around Hemphill Street and Allen Avenue. She seemed to be more of a morning person than a night worker. She had the market for those customers who were on their way to work or on a lunch break.

I met her when I was dispatched to four calls in five days that involved her. This was during a brief time period when I worked day shift patrol. I quickly learned that this woman had a hot temper. As a result, she was often involved in fights, arguments, and assaults with beer bottles. She always had a cigarette burning, always smelled very strongly of alcohol, and most sickeningly, she was always pregnant. During my last conversation with her, she was pregnant with twins.

She had previously given birth to six children. Where were they? Lee Ann gave all six of her children to her mother and asked her mother to raise them. I asked her if she had ever considered birth control, and she said, "No way! I like making babies. They are precious."

I was in disbelief at her lack of concern for the fact that she was bringing these children into the world with the risk of birth defects on a regular basis. She had no regard for the possible detriment she could be causing her unborn children. And further, no regard for her poor mother who was raising all of her kids, as if they were her own.

During this most recent conversation with her when she was pregnant with twins, she was drunk, smoking, and had just recently been fighting with beer bottles. She had a gash across her forehead from the scuffle with a roommate over a "boyfriend." The woman was a complete mess. I asked her what was going to happen to these two babies when she had them. She proudly exclaimed, "Oh that's no problem, my mom will take them."

# Chapter Eight
## Accident Prone

Throughout the years I have earned the reputation with my family and friends of being clumsy and accident prone. My husband says that I could get hurt in a round, padded room. He is right. However, sometimes things happen to people that are beyond control, and I have been able to witness these things first hand. Sometimes they happen to me, and other times they happen to others, but if I am around, they will usually happen to someone! These unusual things don't necessarily always have to encompass pain, but in many instances, they certainly could have ended up that way if things had been just a bit different.

### Nearly Impaled

My first example is one that still makes me cringe, and it happened over twelve years ago. I was working midnight shift patrol, driving down Morningside drive, patrolling my beat. Suddenly, I heard a loud screeching, a clank, and then an unbearable grinding noise. I looked out the window and observed sparks coming from just underneath my door. I had to come to a stop, because the sound was piercing and there was no way I could continue without seeing what was wrong. I turned on my emergency light bar and exited the vehicle. When I looked beneath my car, I was utterly shocked to see that I had run over a long, metal crowbar that had catapulted into the undercarriage of my car, piercing the body of the vehicle. That was bad enough, but when I inspected the *inside* of my car underneath my driver's seat, I was mortified. The crow bar was sticking about three inches into the body of the car, right underneath where I had been sitting. It missed the bottom of my seat by inches! That was one of the creepiest feelings, and I can still remember the relief I felt when I recognized how close that came to possibly impaling me.

Next on my mind was the issue of conquering this problem. It was going to be rather tricky to find a way to remove this thing. Luckily a fellow officer was nearby, and I sent him a message on my mobile data terminal (MDT). I simply said, "Can you make my location?" I could not find it in me to elaborate in my message. I wanted him to see for himself. He wouldn't have believed it, anyway. Upon his arrival, he looked at me and the car, and shook his head. We both pondered how to move the car without further impaling the seat of the car, and possibly the driver. The vehicle had come to rest about ten feet from a curb. We decided that if we jumped the curb a bit, we would have room to dislodge the crowbar.

I moved the car ever-so-gingerly and slowly from the middle of the road up onto the curb. In doing so, the blood-curdling screeching sound was regenerated, and as a result, several people came outside from their homes. Yes, it was the middle of the night, probably around 1:00 a.m. unfortunately. They watched with disbelief as we pulled and jimmied the crowbar to release it from the crumpled metal of the undercarriage of my car. Finally, it came loose, leaving only a small rip to commemorate its wrath. The crow bar did not bend; it was as straight as an arrow. I threw it in the floorboard in case a supervisor needed to see it, in order to believe what had happened. I was thankful and regretful in the same breath that my fellow officer had been able to witness the incident. He just continually shook his head and said, "How in the world did you do that?" I had no good answer for him, other than that I am just me and things like that happen to me.

## Fire Hazard

Another calamity that strongly rivals the crowbar incident is a time when my partner and I were attempting to check an alley for abandoned stolen cars, again on the midnight shift. We often drove through alleyways, which, in Fort Worth, are not common or widespread. In addition to their scarcity, another quality inherent for alleys is the lack of proper maintenance. Alleys normally consist of overgrown patches of tall grass, peppered with old tires, bags of trash, squads of rodents and snakes, and are bordered with fences riddled with graffiti. As a result, these run-down easements provide means of secrecy and mobility for criminals. This leads to the necessity for patrol officers to customarily trudge through and inspect them for any fruits of criminal activity hiding in their midst. The risk of getting a flat tire in an alley is pretty high, but duty calls, so officers regularly take that risk, which pales in comparison to other risks routinely taken in a shift.

My partner and I were making progress about one-third the way through the alley, when suddenly, we heard a thud and a gradual brushing sound that seemed to get closer to us as we eased forward. At first, I thought we had run over a person who might have been sleeping in the alley. However, it quickly became obvious that this item beneath our car was much larger, and much more inclined to hold on than any person would be. This item became wedged perfectly underneath the vehicle. We were in the overgrown alley and neither of us was physically able to exit the vehicle because precisely where we were stopped was dotted with small trees, and we were close to the fence line, too. As a result, we were forced to back out of the alley, and as we did, we began to smell a burning smell, and see some smoke coming from beneath the car. This was seriously scary at this point. My partner gunned the car backward and we dragged the item with us, all the way out of the alley.

When we finally hit the curb line (curbs are very helpful for items lodged underneath vehicles, in case you haven't yet made the connection) the item dislodged itself and we were able to distance ourselves from it. Believe it or not, it was a twin-sized bed mattress that now had the imprint of the catalytic converter and muffler distinctly burning from it. We pulled the mattress into the street, and watched as it burst into flames. We had to call for assistance from the fire department to safely extinguish the mattress. In the meantime, we were laughing uncontrollably, and in the back of our minds, I think we both were emitting a prayer of thanksgiving to God that we were not trapped in the alley, unable to get out of the car, as the entire vehicle became engulfed in flames. Imagine the headlines.

## Mirror Mishap

While my regular partner and I were working together on midnight shift one night, we were in two separate cars. We had finished up a call, and were pulled up next to one another in a parking lot so we could fill out our worksheets. When officers do paperwork, they will customarily pull up with driver's side windows adjacent to one another. This ensures that any subjects approaching on foot or in a vehicle will be visible from all directions.

We were just finishing up when I decided I needed to go check on something nearby. I accelerated, but instead of going forward, I went backward. I suddenly heard a violent crunch, and then shattering glass. That sound is never a good one, especially when you are driving someone else's (for instance, the taxpayers') car. I just knew I had broken the mirror on my patrol vehicle, and I pulled forward again in order to inspect the damage. As I looked over at my partner in the car next to me, I observed the most unforgettably dumbfounded look on his face. I had backed into his side view mirror with my side view mirror. His mirror shattered and shards of glass hit the ground with a clinking sound. However, my mirror was in perfect condition, without a scratch.

Even though I caused the incident, he would receive disciplinary documentation in his file, too. This was unfair, and I felt horrible about it. It was ironic that his car was damaged pretty badly and mine was not damaged at all.

As per our General Orders policy we had to contact a supervisor, who had to come out to the scene and fill out a special report and complete a host of extra paperwork. The crime scene unit had to come out and photograph the damage to the vehicle. My mistake that took approximately one second to carry out had caused three different people about six hours worth of extra work. Bureaucracy at its best was at work here. I realized I had broken the side view mirror, but did we really have to contact the media?

This was really all I needed - another clumsy and stupid thing to try to live down with my team out there on midnight shift. If you would give them something to pounce on, they would pounce. I could only pray that someone else would do something stupid real soon, to get me off the hook! Have no fear – it wasn't long before my dear friend with the broken mirror had a mishap of his own. We will read about that later, and there will be laughing.

# Fall of My Professionalism

    I still laugh when I envision this next mishap, which happened to my midnight shift partner on another occasion when we were riding together. He liked to drive, and I enjoyed doing paperwork, so we worked well together, and we rode together as often as we could. Patrolling our assigned area during this shift we heard a "sexual assault in progress" call go out on Hemphill Street, very close to its intersection with Morningside Drive. It was reportedly occurring in a halfway house on the west side of the street. We were close, so we hailed the dispatcher and took the call. The details stated a man was assaulting a woman inside an apartment unit on the second floor of this building. We were familiar with these rental properties which housed individuals who were phasing out of drug and alcohol addiction programs. There were often relapses which resulted in various types of arguments, violence, and assaults. Usually, however, the calls we received were placed after the fact, and not while any dangerous assault was in progress. This one was a high priority, with a potentially dangerous suspect still on the scene, actively committing the crime.

    We drove up and parked a half block away from the location at a fast food restaurant for safety purposes. We exited the vehicle, and were moving pretty fast. We actually began running towards the front of the building because the call-taker kept receiving updates from the person who was reporting the incident on the telephone inside. As we approached the short three-step stairway that led up the yard in front of the building, we could hear screaming and yelling. Then, as I followed my partner up the stairs, I watched as he tripped and fell. He catapulted himself forward and his knee cap hit one of the concrete stairs dead-on with full force. The pain, I am certain, was beyond excruciating. He hit the ground and began rolling around, writhing in pain. All the while, there were still screams and yelling coming from the second floor breezeway.

    There were some very serious things happening all at once, the most pressing of which was my partner rolling around on the ground incapacitated by pain and a possibly broken knee cap. This was aside from the possibility that there was a rape in progress occurring just thirty feet away, inside the walls of the apartment building.

    It doesn't take much consideration to recognize that this was not the most appropriate time for me to lose my composure and start laughing beyond control. Even so – it happened. I began laughing hysterically. This was one of those laughs that you know is completely unprofessional, out of place, and yet, one that would not stop. This is one of those laughs that I knew could get me into trouble, one that was making my miserable partner very angry, and worst of all, one that could have gotten us both killed!

I knew I had to get on the radio and call for more help. The highest priority had become my partner, who was seriously injured and completely helpless. This is one of those situations they warn you about where the officer brings a gun to the call, and if he or she is unable to secure it, then the danger to all involved exponentially increases. He was not unconscious, but he was in bad enough shape that I dared not leave him out there alone. All of this was exacerbated terribly by the fact that I was still unable to stop laughing, and my face was now red with tears pouring from my eyes. I could barely get the words out of my mouth to transmit on the radio that we needed an ambulance. The dispatcher could detect that something was wrong with me. So could the other officers.

My injured partner was extremely angry with me. He was my friend, and I was laughing at him as he lay on the ground in miserable pain. I knew this, it made me feel really bad, but even still, I could not stop laughing at the sight of him tripping, flying, and landing on that stair step with his knee. It was quite a feat, and I would have given anything to have been able to videotape it. If he could have seen it himself at a later time maybe he would be able to understand why it struck me as being so funny - then again, maybe not.

By the grace of God alone (as was the case daily during my career), a second and third unit drove up almost immediately. I had just explained over the radio that my partner needed an ambulance, so other officers heard that transmission and came to assist us, wondering what had happened. As I stood there laughing completely unprofessionally, I was actually incapacitated as well. The new officers on the scene went up stairs into the apartment building to check on our original crisis. Upon arrival, they found that there had never really been a sexual assault, at all. Actually, it had been just a verbal dispute between two neighbors, a man and a woman, who were both intoxicated. The call had been made by a fellow tenant who heard the yelling and embellished the report to the call taker. The man had already gone back to his room and shut himself in for the night. The woman was angry, but she was not in any danger whatsoever. This was pretty normal stuff for the halfway houses along Hemphill Street. Unfortunately, the embellishment of facts by this caller ultimately caused my partner to bust his leg up. He went to the hospital for X-rays. While he had not cracked the bone, he had impacted his knee quite badly, and had to be off work for a couple of days.

When he finally returned to roll call after missing a few days of work, I approached him to see how he was doing. He gave me the angriest and most disgusted look one could ever imagine. He was still very angry with me. He had cursed at me on the scene of the accident, a few nights before, while I laughed at him. He could not figure out why I was laughing at him while he was hurting so badly. All I could muster up to say to him was "I'm sorry." This was in between my attempts to take a breath during my heaving laughter. That night, his angry cursing had only fueled my laughter more. I had acted unprofessionally, and I realized I had also strained our working relationship.

I was barely able to get him to listen to me as I tried to explain my behavior. Then the worst happened. I started laughing again. I could not even look at him without bursting into a belly laugh. Then he cursed at me again, and I knew that I deserved it. I didn't lose control this time, and was able to stop laughing pretty soon after absorbing the piercing look of anger on his face. I apologized sincerely. I had to explain to him that he had just made such an athletic catapult into the air that I had been overcome by surprise at his hidden abilities. He accepted my apology, but he was still a bit angry with me about it. As a matter of fact, even years later when I would run across him in passing, I would think of that night. I would bring it up, laughing, and he would laugh a little bit, too. Then, he would curse at me and call me the same name he had adopted for me that night as I stood over him laughing at his mishap.

## Crash

When I worked midnight shift, my favorite area became the neighborhood near Hemphill Street and Allen Avenue. This is because I had trained in the area on dayshift, and I knew the residents and other citizens who frequented the area. Also, there was a convenience store on the corner where officers would meet to stay adequately supplied with

81

soda and snacks (not donuts). For me, the place was my source of soda and chocolate. These were two of the important supplies I needed in order to do good police work.

One night in 1992, very early in my career, I was working in that favorite neighborhood. I decided to take a break to get a drink, so I headed for my regular convenience store. That decision almost cost me my life. If it hadn't been for God's activation of one of those force fields I mentioned earlier, I can only imagine how things would have been. God provided that armor for my protection at precisely the right moment in order to prevent my sustaining some very serious injuries (or even some deadly ones).

I was heading northbound in the 1600 Block of Hemphill Street, approaching the traffic light at its intersection with Allen Avenue. My light was green, so I proceeded through the intersection as I had done, nonchalantly, so many times before. There is a concrete wall erected on the southwest corner of that intersection which renders it nearly impossible to see any oncoming vehicles from that direction.

In a split second, I saw bright headlights moving towards the driver's side of my car at a dangerously rapid pace. All of a sudden, a red truck slammed into my patrol vehicle at full speed. The driver had not even attempted to stop at his red traffic light. I am quite certain that it is by the grace of God alone, once again, that I was protected from more serious injury. The impact hit my car directly on the front left wheel, and annihilated the front end of my cruiser. It was later determined that the driver was travelling in excess of 60 mph when he hit my car.

The airbag deployed in front of me as the sound of the impact resonated throughout the passenger compartment of the car. All I could see was the white wall of cloth and a cloud of smoke in my face. I actually thought that I had died, and was floating into the unknown realm of glorious white light and the puffy cotton clouds of heaven. However, I quickly realized that this was not heaven, because the pain was too great. My flashlight, which had been in the seat next to my right thigh, turned perpendicular to my leg during the crash and nearly impaled me. I felt a sharp and throbbing pain emanating through my entire right side. Simultaneously my entire body had been thrust upward and backward into the metal cage that was mounted between my seat and the back passenger compartment. This cage was bolted to the frame of the car, so when there was an impromptu battle between me and the metal cage, I did not win. My neck and spine seemed to expand and then contract like an accordion.

When the car stopped spinning and finally came to rest up against the light pole in the northeast corner of the intersection, I had sustained a whiplash, a concussion, a badly bruised leg, and the beginning of a bronchial infection from the dust in the air bag. The equipment inside my car had been destroyed, including my brand new briefcase that had been provided by the Department just a few months earlier during graduation from the academy. It had been impacted so hard by the interior of the car that it disintegrated. As a result, all of my equipment, paperwork and personal items flew chaotically throughout the inside of the car.

Due to its speed and velocity, the truck that hit me continued eastbound on Allen for about a half of a block, and finally came to rest up against a fence which bordered a nearby parking lot. The driver was in the vehicle, barely injured. Over time I would learn that when a driver was extremely intoxicated and /or high he or she could endure the trauma of an impact much better than someone who was not. This man had been arrested three previous times for driving while intoxicated, and on this night, he was also under the influence of prescription drugs. As a matter of fact, it was determined that he had an extensive criminal history involving drugs and alcohol. Apparently he was so impaired that he had disregarded at least three stop signs on Allen Avenue before hitting my car at the intersection. That is the only way he could have been going so fast upon impact with me.

Two of my colleagues were parked in the lot at the convenience store finishing up some paperwork and waiting for me to arrive. Both of them witnessed the crash as it happened directly in front of them. They both sprang into action immediately. They checked on me, called for an ambulance, and apprehended the driver who had hit me.

Citizens began to gather at the intersection to look at the crashed vehicles. Because we were so close to the hospital district, an ambulance arrived very quickly. I was hurting pretty badly, and was unsure as to the extent of my injuries because the pain was constant and potent. The adrenaline was really pumping, but I could still feel the pain - sharp, violent pain. As a result, I went to the hospital in an ambulance for the first time in my life.

*This is my patrol vehicle after the front end was practically ripped away by a severely impaired driver. When I look at these photos it becomes clear that God was protecting me that night. If I had travelled just a few feet further, the impact would have been at my driver's side door. My injuries would have been much worse, if not fatal.*

I had worked quite a few accidents even by this point early in my career. I had accompanied many crash victims into the back of an ambulance to gather information for their accident reports. However, until I was the one on that rickety rolling metal cot, I really never quite understood how intimidating the process could be. The paramedics were extremely helpful and made me feel very comfortable. Even so, I felt a loss of control that made me feel very uneasy. I left the scene with the lights on in the back of the ambulance, knowing that anyone who pulled up in a vehicle behind us could see me sitting there, vulnerable, in pain, in the back of that truck. Luckily we were close to Harris Methodist Hospital, which is where they took me for my treatment.

My colleagues had secured all of my personal things and some other officers had arrived on the scene from the Traffic division to work the crash, because my City vehicle was involved. It was very beneficial to have those two fellow officers there who had witnessed the accident, because that helped solidify the fact that I was not at fault. This meant that I would not be disciplined for this incident departmentally. However, that did not exempt me from other punishment. I suffered irreversible muscle damage and still to this day I have muscle spasms in my right shoulder, which cause migraine headaches. I was off work for several days as a result of what I thought was normal soreness, before I reported for duty again.

## My Biggest Mistake

When I returned to work I remained in patrol for a few months before I was transferred into the Traffic Division, specifically the D.W.I. (Driving While Intoxicated) Unit. I accepted a position in Traffic because I felt most comfortable with the task of monitoring and evaluating traffic for intoxicated drivers. This was something I had learned to do well, and because of my gross lack of experience in other types of police work, I felt this was my forte, at least for the time being.

After a while I began to have migraine headaches and uncontrollable muscle spasms in my right shoulder on a regular basis. This stemmed from the on-duty crash I had been involved in several months earlier. Even though it had been a while, I knew the pain was a direct result of that crash. Pretty soon the headaches and the muscle spasms became so severe that I had to return to my doctor.

I explained my symptoms, and he agreed that the heavy protective vest and the leather gear we had to carry on our person each shift further aggravated the injury. These items were essential for my work, and there was no alternative to wearing them. The crash, which had occurred several months earlier, was clearly still causing me problems. As a result, the doctor provided me with some medication for my pain and the muscle spasms.

Even though I was still in a lot of pain, I felt a responsibility, both to myself and the Department, to move forward and do my job. I had never been hurt badly in a car wreck before, and did not realize that the impact would take its toll on the body for more than just a few days, weeks or months. I did not take medications often, so I hadn't used many of the muscle relaxers or pain medication before this time. Instead I just began to sleep excessively. I began to feel desperate, and the return visit to my doctor had provided some hope for relief. I certainly could not continue to function like I had been.

One night as I began to get ready for work, I was feeling particularly bad, but I knew I had to go in to work. Because the doctor had provided me with the medication to numb my pain, I figured if I took it, I would feel better. I hoped it would make subsequent shifts back at work wearing that miserable vest and the heavy equipment more bearable. As a result, I took a dose of each prescription and took a nap. Then, when I awoke, I took another dose and headed to work, reporting for roll call as usual.

I had slept quite a bit since my doctor's appointment. When the alarm clock sounded that evening it had been really hard to wake up. I even felt dizzy. I figured this was because I had been sleeping so much. I felt lethargic and my body felt unusually heavy when I tried to move. It took extra effort for me to do anything at all. It was really difficult for me to function. I was in a funk, and I needed to shake it, fast. Even so, I made it to work, thinking I would eventually feel more awake and alert.

Somehow I made it through roll call, too. I placed my equipment in the patrol vehicle and headed to the south side, which was my assigned area to patrol for those dangerous drivers who were under the influence. Little did I know I needed look no further than in my own rearview mirror to find someone who was unfit to drive!

I stopped a traffic violator at the intersection of Rosedale and 1-35 on the way to the south side of town. While I was approaching the driver, I felt very dizzy and lethargic. I realized that I was in no shape to be out approaching an unknown violator in a perilous neighborhood at 11:00 p.m. I was actually in a lot of danger. I approached his window and asked for his driver's license. He told me he did not have it. Instead of prodding further as I normally would have, I explained to the man that his rear tail light was out. I told him to drive carefully and to get that corrected as soon as possible. I returned to my vehicle, and thanked God for protecting me as I had just entered the roadway and approached this stranger without my full bearings. I was impaired, and I was not functioning well at all.

After I let this man go, I drove about three miles further to the fire station at 3300 Hemphill Street to get fuel in my car. I kept wrestling with the choices I had to make. I could wait this out and try to function without my full mental capacity, or I could notify my sergeant that I had made a terrible mistake and risk getting into big trouble for driving this far while being impaired.

I exited my patrol car to fill up with gas. As I inserted my fuel-key into the keypad, I realized that I could not even punch the correct code numbers into the keypad. I kept hitting the wrong number and seeing the "access denied" flash up on the screen.

This is when I realized that I simply had to call my sergeant because I was completely unable to function safely. As a matter of fact, I was as bad, or worse than some of the drunk drivers I routinely arrested. The only difference between me and those suspects I routinely arrested was that they chose to drive knowing they had been ingesting a mind altering substance, and I had taken medication which had affected me in ways I did not anticipate. Even so, this was no excuse.

When I contacted my sergeant, he came to my location and spoke with me. He was upset that I had driven that far feeling the way I did. I explained to him that I did not expect the feeling to last, and I didn't really realize it was from my prescription until I was already conducting a traffic stop. He and another officer arranged to get me and my patrol vehicle back to the sector, and they took me home. This was a Saturday night, and the following Monday I visited my doctor again. He advised me that I needed to take this medicine for awhile to allow my body to heal. If I could not function at work after taking it, I would need to stay home from work. As a result, I ended up being off work for several months on disability. During this time, I took my medication, in addition to several steroid shots to my shoulder, and physical therapy. When it was time to return to work several months later, believe me, I did not take any medication before roll call. I still have problems with my neck and shoulder even fifteen years after the fact. I can only thank God that I was not hurt worse. Furthermore, I shudder at the thought of what could have happened without God's protection when I took my medication and went to work. I am so thankful that I did not make a mistake that caused harm to me or to someone else. God is my protector, and as always He carried me through during a potentially dangerous situation.

## Elusive Hungry Black Dog

Early in my career I seemed prone to car crashes. Only two years after the bad crash I detailed before, I was involved in another one. This time, however, it was my fault. One morning at about 4:45 a.m., I was headed eastbound on Hwy 121 approaching Beach Street. It had been a long and busy shift, and I was heading to the east side to have breakfast with some of my fellow officers at our favorite 24-hour restaurant. At the time, I was working the Traffic Division, in the D.W.I. (Driving While Intoxicated) Unit. We were allowed to travel across district lines in the course of our duties, which included patrolling the entire City watching for dangerously impaired drivers. I had been working in the North division during this shift, and consequently had to drive quite a distance to meet my colleagues.

As I crested the bridge which crossed over Fairview Avenue below, I observed a medium sized black dog in the middle lane of the freeway. This dog was sitting there, eating food that had been thrown out onto the roadway from another vehicle. I could identify the fast food restaurant from which the food came, and could even see that the dog was eating chicken bones that were in the bag. This was possible because I was also in the middle lane, travelling about sixty-five miles per hour.

While I am an animal lover, and would never have wanted to hit that poor dog, I must admit that the decision I made at the time is not one that I would replicate, knowing what I know now. I didn't have time to think about avoiding this poor animal, because my instincts kicked in, and I quickly veered to the right, causing a jerking action. My vehicle entered into the slow lane – for a fraction of a second. However, I hit the brake pretty hard at the same time. As a result, I spun around two or three times, heading towards the center median concrete wall. I hit the wall with three different corners of my patrol vehicle, which was still spinning.

When my vehicle finally came to rest, I was facing westbound in the eastbound fast lane of the freeway. My car was disabled, and I could not move it. I remember being stunned from the several impacts with the wall. Thankfully, I never hit another vehicle, because the only other vehicle out on the road was a witness who had been behind me. I had the presence of mind to activate my emergency light bar on top of my car. I prayed that no one would crest that hill and hit me head-on. The witness who was behind me just happened to be a media photographer from a local news station. He stopped on the median and came to my assistance. I had already gotten on the radio and called for another unit and a supervisor.

Unfortunately, the very officers I intended to have breakfast with were the ones summonsed to work the accident that I had just caused. The dog was pretty smart. He high-tailed it off the roadway after hearing the several crashes resounding around him. During the process he grabbed a chicken bone from the discarded trash in the road and disappeared, never to be seen again.

I had two things going for me. First of all, the remainder of the fast-food bag was still in the roadway, obviously torn open. This helped support my story that the elusive "black dog" had really existed. Furthermore, the news photographer stayed on the scene until my supervisor arrived, and relayed what he had seen. He reported seeing the big black dog in the middle of the road, and seeing me swerve to miss him, and then watching me spinning into the crash. Thank God for him! He saved my tail.

It was later determined that I had sustained over $13,000 worth of damage to that City vehicle. My supervisor, who would have normally fought for the maximum punishment in this type of situation, actually advocated leniency for me. It was recommended by some higher up that I get two days off without pay for my careless action that had resulted in such extensive and expensive damage. However, with the witness statement, my statement, and my supervisor's advocacy, ultimately, I ended up with only a written reprimand placed in my file. This was a huge break. This could have cost me some time off without pay. However, by the grace of God, again, I was not injured, and my penalty for a huge mistake was very minimal. Even so, I learned a lesson about swerving to miss animals in the roadway, and developed a new philosophy, as well. Basically, if you are an animal in the road, and you are in front of me while I am driving, you can either run fast to get out of my way, or you can kiss your fuzzy tail goodbye!

*At the beginning of my career I tended to be a bit rough on vehicles. Here you can see the ridiculous amount of damage I caused when I swerved to miss a stray dog on the freeway. Thank God there was a witness or no one would have ever believed me!*

## Terrible Takeoff

As bad as my luck with cars seemed to be, everyone should thank God that I never tried to fly an aircraft. Never fear, though! I would never be able to complete that type of training because my personal fear of crashing due to a mechanical malfunction would prove too great for me to overcome. Despite my seemingly irrational fear of these unlikely events, they were somewhat reinforced one November day when the Careflight crew in Fort Worth had a rough takeoff and ended up in a pretty outrageous predicament.

I was working at my alternative high school just down the street from Harris Methodist Hospital in downtown Fort Worth, when I heard via police radio that a helicopter had crashed on the roof of the hospital. Actually, the helicopter did not crash per-se. It did, however, experience a very hard landing while the pilot worked to correct a botched takeoff attempt. The rotors clipped a metal pole and caused debris to fly off of the tenth floor rooftop of the hospital and onto the ground below. The crippled copter was left sitting just along the edge of the helipad.

Trimble Tech High School is literally across the street from the hospital, and several students were outside walking during the time of the mishap. When the pilot experienced trouble, the copter bobbled, causing its tail rotor to hit the metal pole and disintegrate. Pieces of the aircraft went flying indiscriminately onto the street below, and onto the grassy lawn of the high school. Students were stunned, and citizens who saw the remnants of this near tragic accident were amazed that it was not worse.

Officers were recruited to block off the roadways while the appropriate investigations were conducted. The National Transportation Safety Board and the Federal Aviation Administration had to send out investigators to document the events of this mishap. This surprisingly minor incident was dangerously close to being a major tragedy. I remember reporting to my post, where I was directed to handle traffic control. When I arrived, I saw various pieces of painted metal scattered about. When I looked up, I was mortified to see the helicopter sitting near the edge of the concrete roof of the hospital, with the tail rotor completely destroyed. It appeared as if the aircraft had almost fallen off of the edge.

This was the same heroic helicopter crew that would routinely rescue those in dire need of medical attention. My heart fluttered with horror as I thought of the pilot, flight nurse and medic who normally take care of others in need. Today, however, they were the ones in the position of danger. At the time we were not sure if there were any injuries to the crew or the passengers, although we learned soon that this was one of the times when God put a force-field over the whole scene. The people onboard, as well as those below on the ground were all safe. I could not help but think of what could have happened.

This had the potential to be a tragic accident, except for the few feet of concrete up on that roof, and the providence of God. If the pilot had experienced his problem just yards in either direction, the situation could have turned grizzly. The fact that there were no serious injuries was miraculous, considering the number of people who were walking in the area down below the minor crash. Drivers maneuvered through the area as students and citizens walked below the scene in this normally bustling, high traffic area of the community. However, due to the expertise of that pilot, along with the providence of God, once again, a tragedy was averted. Even though things worked out okay, I still don't see myself ever applying to flight school.

# Chapter Nine
## Incredible Desperation

Life can be rough for all of us at times, and day to day stresses can take a toll on people's ability to make rational decisions. Relationship problems, arguments, financial problems, employment issues, family troubles, disease or illness, addiction, and the combination of any of these can lead to incredible desperation when the symptoms conglomerate without treatment. People who are suffering these types of issues often need professional therapeutic guidance in order to return to a normal balance in life.

When symptoms are not treated, resulting irrational decisions can have rash consequences. Just as the young man in my opening segment tried to end his life by taking a combination of dangerous substances, others sometimes explore different methods to attempt this very final solution to their temporary problems. Sometimes desperation can propel people into circumstances where likely consequences are not even considered until after the fact. In this segment I will detail the results of some of these situations.

### Jumper
*[This story contains mild undesirable language]*

An attempt at creative personal disposal was evidenced one night while I was working the far deep Southside beat. I was dispatched to a report of a man who was standing up on the highest overpass in the City. He was on the ramp of westbound I-20 leading to southbound I-35. He had parked his car nearby on the median, and had walked over to the highest point, which overlooked the freeway below. He was sitting on the wall, his feet hanging over, facing about a 120 foot drop to the hard pavement of the unsuspecting freeway below. This gentleman had a plan. He was going to jump off of this bridge. His life was a mess, and he was having a seemingly impossible disagreement with his wife. He was in desperation, with tears running down his face.

I must disclose to you now that one of my worst fears in this life is the fear of heights. As a result, I was not quite at ease, myself. I was the first officer to arrive on the scene. I pulled up and blocked the roadway partially by angling my patrol vehicle towards the retaining wall. I turned on my emergency light bar. Before I exited the car, I breathed a brief but sincere prayer to God, requesting His guidance. I was about twenty feet from this man, who was approximately 120 feet from his death.

I exited my car slowly. I was barely able to move. I immediately began feeling vertigo from just being up on the ramp. I knew this was a sensitive situation for this man. If he was going to jump, I didn't want it to be because I startled him. As tragic as it would be, if he did jump, it needed to be his decision. I addressed him with the most heartfelt sincerity I could muster in my state of terror.

"Sir, please lean backward and get off of that railing. Please don't fall. Please don't jump."

In the back of my mind was the knowledge that other officers and a supervisor were on the way. These are the kinds of calls that usually merit a trained negotiator. I wanted this to end quickly, and with a positive outcome, without having to call in the cavalry at 2:30 a.m.

"I want to die," the man yelled to me in a painfully sincere voice.

"I know you think you feel that way right now – but that is such a final decision to make when you are so emotional and feeling badly about things. Please come off of that wall!"

"I need to die. I am scared to jump, but I need to."

During this exchange I was still standing right by the door to my patrol vehicle. I was trying to find a way to convince him to come off of the wall without my having to approach him. I didn't want to spook him, and I didn't want him to take me with him, either. An idea flashed into my mind. Having known several people throughout the course of my life who were confined to a wheelchair, and also knowing that those people obviously did not choose to be in that position, I related that possibility to the man. I regret to this day that my presentation was so crude. Even so, I know God prompted me in this, because I would have never thought of it on my own. If I had it to do all over again, I would probably refrain from using such profane imagery. However, I did it, and I cannot change that fact. As a result, I must admit that without much time to think things through I spoke to him sternly, in an almost mean and mocking voice.

"You know – if you jump off of that wall and hit the ground, you may not die. Sometimes people don't. It is not high enough. If you break your neck, you will be paralyzed. You will be in a wheelchair for the rest of your life and someone will have to wipe your ass for you. Do you think that would be any way to live - especially if you think you have problems now?"

The man looked at me with disbelief. I was surprised at what had come out of my mouth, but he was pondering what I said. I felt for a moment that I had been a bit disrespectful, but this man clearly needed something to get his attention. This exchange was something he was not expecting from the officer who was trying to "save him" when he may not have wanted to be saved.

"Just lean backward. You will only fall about three feet. Then roll over and crawl to me. I will take you to get some help. Please, let me help you. You know you really need someone to listen to you right now. I will listen. I promise. Please come over to me!"

I certainly was not going to approach him. I cared for the guy, but if he was really ready to die, he might not mind taking a companion along with him. I told him the truth about me.

"I am very afraid of heights. This is very uncomfortable for me, but I am here because I care about you. Please!"

I could see the flashing lights of two more police cars approaching in the distance. One was my assist officer and the other was my sergeant. They were still some distance away, but from where I was perched up on the tallest stretch of roadway in the City I could see them, five minutes before they would arrive. I warned the man.

"Look, there are other officers coming. My supervisor will make a big deal out of this situation. He will send me away and call a negotiator. I won't be able to listen to you tell me about what's going on. Let's end this danger for you now. Please, come over to me, and you can be in the car before they ever get here."

He had already been thinking about what I had said before. Although it seemed like an hour, actually within about a minute and a half from the time I arrived the man leaned backward, rolled over, and crawled towards me. I directed him to remain on the roadway and come closer to me, slowly. He did as I asked him to. I handcuffed him securely and helped him up. I could see the relief in his eyes. I could feel his heart beating triple time. He was as scared as I was. I patted him down for weapons and then placed him, carefully, into the back of my car.

About the time my car door closed, my supervisor drove up behind me. I relayed the events to him, and advised him that the man had obeyed my directives to come away from the wall. I explained that the gentleman was in emotional distress, and needed to be transported to the local hospital for a mental evaluation. He seemed somewhat impressed that I had been able to accomplish a positive outcome for this situation. We would not need to wake up the negotiator team tonight. However, he did contact a family member that could come and pick up the man's car for him. He handled that aspect of the situation for me so that I could transport the gentleman to the hospital.

On the way, we talked quite a bit. I explained to him that before I ever got out of the car I had prayed for him, begging God to allow me to say the right words to change his mind about jumping. He laughed and said, "Well, you certainly have a way with words." I laughed, too, and we both shared a brief moment of tension filled laughter.

I apologized for my language and then I listened as he told me about some of the issues going on between him and his wife. He vented during the twenty minute trip to the hospital. After we arrived, I transferred him to the custody of the hospital staff while I completed my paperwork. After the doctor signed the application for mental detention, I said goodbye to the man, and told him I would continue to pray for him. He smiled at me, and thanked me for my kindness. As I left, I felt as if somehow things would get better for him in the days to come.

## "Minty-Fresh" Drunk
*[This story depicts alcoholism]*

Sometimes the desperate behaviors of people do not necessarily indicate a wish to commit suicide. This account will tell about one of those times. For instance, early in a shift one night when I was working midnight patrol I drove up onto the scene where a man was passed out on the sidewalk in the 2000 block of Hemphill Street. Although it was not uncommon to find intoxicated transients passed out in the area, it was unusual to see them while they still had possession of their property, before it was stolen by another transient.

This man had a backpack which was on the ground right next to his. I approached him very carefully, having learned lessons about disturbing drunks from deep sleep (as you will read about later in "*A Case for the Taser*"). I could tell that he was barely breathing, and his breaths were very sporadic and infrequent. I checked his pulse, and found it was weak and slow. I was not able to feel it well from his wrist, so I checked his carotid artery along the side of his neck. It was somewhat stronger there, but not much.

I was somewhat concerned for this man, because he appeared to be deeply under the influence of some type of depressant or very strong liquor. I opened his backpack to check for some identification or maybe an address of a nearby relative or friend. Inside was a pair of socks, a belt, and a plastic bag from the nearby dollar store. The plastic bag contained three empty trial-sized bottles of mouthwash and two empty bottles of rubbing alcohol. There was still one full bottle of rubbing alcohol in the bag, as well, and a receipt. The time on the receipt showed to be earlier that day.

It was then that it hit me what this man had done. When he ran out of liquor he was desperate for some other type of cheap alcohol to drink. He went to the dollar store and spent two dollars on six bottles of merchandise that contained alcohol - *any type of alcohol.* Apparently the man had consumed the contents of these bottles. There was no other obvious explanation for them being in his things.

I feared the man had poisoned himself, so I called the MedStar ambulance to check him out. When the paramedics arrived on the scene, they were able to use ammonia capsules to wake the man up. They checked his vitals and spoke with him after he recovered from the foul odor of the capsules. The man confirmed to them that he had drunk the bottles throughout the day. He boasted that he had done it before, and he was clearly not concerned about the effects this type of substance might have on his body. Ultimately, the man refused medical treatment and the ambulance left. This is just another testament to the lengths some people will go to improvise in a pinch.

After having him medically cleared, I ended up taking him to the "detox" tank at the jail so he could safely sober up without laying vulnerably in the middle of a sidewalk on Hemphill Street. As I transported him to the jail, I couldn't help but notice that the confines of my small passenger compartment began to fill with a clean, crisp aroma. Unlike the disgusting rank breath that most officers have to tolerate when transporting drunks, I was pleasantly surprised to find that my drunk had extremely fresh, minty breath!

## Pursuit of Pavement

Desperation can manifest itself within a split second. This can happen when a person seems to be minding his or her business, and suddenly the glow of red and blue lights begins to illuminate the space behind the back windshield. One night, those lights proved to be a bit too much for one man, who was being stopped by my former midnight shift training officer. I often partnered up with this officer, because he and I had gotten along so well during my training. I still enjoyed learning from him, even after I was cut loose and working solo patrol. We were in separate cars, on this night, but we were working the same area together between calls.

He initiated a traffic stop on the far south side of town. He ran the license plate on a vehicle, and the computer indicated that the registered owner possibly had warrants. The driver pulled over, and as my partner approached the driver's side window to investigate this possibility, the driver gunned the accelerator and took off. The chase was on. I was now an assist to a pursuit, which completely surprised both of us. It happens from time to time, but we were taken aback by this man's decision to run from us over what appeared to be a couple of traffic warrants.

As we wound through the nearly abandoned streets in the middle of the night on a weeknight, the risk level was pretty low. Since there were not a lot of cars out on the road, our supervisor allowed the pursuit to continue. We entered the ramp onto Interstate 20, eastbound. The driver then took the Oak Grove Road exit. He turned left, and drove onto the bridge which went over I-20. Then something bizarre happened. The driver abandoned his car. He slammed his door open and jumped from the car, leaving it running. This happens routinely, but what happened next does not.

He ran to the guard railing that overlooked the west bound traffic lanes of the Interstate 20 freeway. He hesitated for a brief moment before jumping over it. My partner and I were dumbfounded. This was a drop of at least thirty feet onto the fast lanes of a major freeway. This man was not simply trying to escape; he was trying to take his life – all over some traffic warrants.

Mortified, we both ran to the edge of the railing, and looked down to see him flailing around on the concrete roadway below. We immediately called for other officers and an ambulance. We watched with dread as he lay in the traffic lane, knowing that any second a vehicle could approach, unable to see in the dark of night, and run over this man. Unfortunately, there was no way we could get down to him with a vehicle in timely manner from where we were. All we could do was watch, report his status, and hope the other officers made it to the scene down there before an eighteen wheeler did.

By no logical explanation other than miraculous, divine intervention, the ambulance arrived before he was hit by a car. Even so, he had already sustained major injuries. He had broken both of his legs in several places, aside from sustaining internal injuries. The man survived, but he had substantially compounded his problems by making a series of bad decisions. Instead of simply dealing with a couple of traffic warrants, now he lay in the hospital in very serious condition. In addition, his car had to be towed and stored.

All things considered, this man should have bought a lottery ticket. His luck was stellar. I realize he had some major injuries, but the likelihood of him surviving that ordeal without having been hit by a car was astronomically against his favor. It was evident that God had something in store for him, because he had tried everything in his power to end his life, and that night, it just wasn't meant to happen.

## Organized Exit
*[This story contains graphic and disturbing material]*

During my evening shift training phase when I had only been

out on the streets for a few weeks, my regular training officer was out on personal business. As a result, I was assigned to a different officer for one shift. This officer worked an area that was quite a bit further south than I normally worked. I was not familiar with the area, so he helped me maneuver during the shift by driving. We had a relatively uneventful day and were about an hour from the end of shift when a disturbing call was dispatched into the Lincolnshire neighborhood, which was included in the beat district where we were assigned. The call was a shooting. Sketchy details reported a female who had been shot in the head. Without much more information, my training officer began to run code three, which meant lights, sirens, and increased speed.

En route he drilled me on safety procedures, scenarios, radio protocol, and reporting information that I needed to be especially aware of when we arrived on this scene. This was the first call I had handled where there was actually the possibility of imminent danger involved. We screeched to a halt in front of the home and observed the Med Star ambulance and an engine full of Fort Worth Firefighters that were staging down the road from the address, while waiting for us. They drove up behind us and we headed for the door.

We cautiously approached the front of the home and were met by a male subject before we could enter. Even though he was inconsolably distraught, we had to secure him for our safety. We still did not have any idea what had occurred, including who had been shot, if the shooter was still on scene, and the location of the weapon. We placed cuffs on the man and patted him down. He was writhing around in uncontrollable despair. We asked him the fewest possible questions to ascertain that the scene was safe, and that there was no further danger for anyone in the home. He told us that his ex-wife, who I will call Felicia, had taken her life. It was immediately clear that he was telling us the truth. We quickly released him, apologized for the inconvenience and allowed him to grieve as he well deserved to do. He understood we were only doing our jobs although he was visibly shaken and wrought with disbelief.

It didn't take much more than a glance at the dining room bar to realize that this shooting was no accident. I will describe what I saw there a bit later. The man advised us that this home belonged to his ex-wife. She had called him and asked him to come over and get their dog, to take care of him. The man did not understand why he had received this call until he arrived. When he did, he found Felicia in the bathroom, in the bathtub, dead from a self-inflicted gunshot wound to her right temple.

My training officer prodded me to move towards the bathroom in order for us to inspect the scene, there. I did not want to see this. I was beginning to feel physically ill. The real pain of loss was overcoming me, as a result of the despair this family member was showing in the other room. I prayed for him. I prayed so earnestly that I became a bit emotionally distraught, myself. I realized this was unacceptable since I needed to handle this crisis professionally, so I quickly pulled myself together.

This was one of the hardest things I had ever been forced to see. I will never forget the feeling, realizing this woman's incredible lack of hope, seeing the horrific sights, smelling the smell of blood, and trying to control the sick feeling in my stomach. After all, I had only been out in the field for a couple of weeks. I had never been in any other situation like this. I was holding in an assortment of unfamiliar emotions in order to make it through the rest of this shift and complete my responsibilities.

I was most disturbed by the implication I gathered after looking into the bathtub. The woman's body was still in the tub, clothed in a bathrobe. She looked peacefully non-affected by all the commotion around her. At least now she did. I could see the .380 pistol was still in the tub, right near her right hand. However, there was shocking and gruesome proof that the shot to Felicia's temple had not immediately killed her. There was evidence pointing to an unsuccessful struggle by Felicia to grasp at the pistol, which had fallen from her hand when she fired the shot. There were bloody streaks on the side of the tub, which clearly shadowed the silhouette of the bloody fingers of her right hand. This indicated she was trying for quite some time to find and grasp the pistol so she could try another shot to end her misery. The implications of this were stunning. This meant that Felicia had laid there in pain, fear, and desperation, trying to feel for the pistol so she could accelerate the slow bleeding that was also only *slowly killing* her. She had intended for this to be quick.

Seeing all of this, I wondered if she had wanted to change her mind after the first shot did not kill her instantly. I wondered how long she had been alive after the shot. I wondered what type of desperation she was feeling during the entire process. As I write this nearly fifteen years after it happened, I still feel the sickening and desperate sadness that overcame me that night. I feel it, again, right now, as much as I felt that night, so many years ago.

This was an extremely traumatic experience for me from every angle. There were several factors that contributed to my difficulty in coping with this scene. This was my first deceased person, and knowing that she had suffered a slow and painful death had exponentially increased my distress. Secondly, the victim's ex-husband was heartbroken, and I felt a deep and sincere empathy for him. Thirdly, when I later heard the story behind this woman's desperation that led to her suicide, I could barely restrain myself from sobbing.

The paramedics were charged with the task of verifying Felicia was indeed deceased. In order to appropriately evaluate her they were forced to remove her from the tub, dragging her onto the carpeted floor of the nearby living room. They did not have the room to maneuver around in the bathroom because it was so small. When they moved her body, the blood streaked across the floor, leaving a horrifying trail of crimson stain throughout the bathroom, the hallway, and onto the living room floor. This heightened the despair of the ex-husband. The sheer amount of blood present confirmed the finality of this person's life. This was especially painful to see. It was also clear that this woman had taken the utmost pride in the orderliness and cleanliness of her home, and she did not intend for her suicide to lead to this bloody mess all throughout her house.

As per protocol, we contacted our supervisor, the homicide detectives, and the Crime Scene Search Unit (CSSU). After our determination that the wound was indeed self-inflicted, we awaited the Crime Scene Search Unit's arrival to process the scene. They would collect the weapon and any evidence needed to adequately document the incident.

While we were waiting, things only got worse. The investigation brought to light a devastatingly sad course of events. According to the ex-husband, Felicia was facing a very risky brain surgery to remove a large tumor. She had been told that there was a forty percent chance that the surgery would leave her in a vegetative state. She was very concerned about the likelihood of her family members being burdened with her care. She did not want them to have to do this. As a result, she made what she felt was a selfless decision to take her life in order to alleviate any possibility of becoming a burden to her loved ones.

Not quite recognizing that her family really wanted her alive, regardless of the outcome of the surgery, Felicia had made the decision to end her life. Giving more evidence of her loving and accommodating character, this woman had painstakingly organized all of her effects in order to make her estate manageable for her family.

First of all, as was evidenced when we initially walked through the front door, she had written a separate personal note for each of about seven family members. Every note was systematically placed face-up on the bar, lined up in a very orderly fashion. On each note was a piece of jewelry or some other special possession that was significant for the person to whom the note was written. For instance, one note was written to a niece, and on top of it were a couple of rings that Felicia wanted this young girl to have. There were six other similar letters, each graced with a piece of what had formerly been Felicia's life.

In one very lengthy note to her ex-husband, Felicia had included details of her finances. She included all of her credit card bills, personal documents, checkbooks, account numbers, insurance policies, payment books, and anything else she could think of that would make things easier for those left behind to deal with her affairs. She even included her file from the dog's veterinarian. This was the dog that she and her ex-husband had shared.

She had written out checks for each of the bills that were due, and had placed them in stamped envelopes. This was so it would be clear which bills were paid and which were not. She had tried to think of everything. She was so concerned about making things "easy" for her family. If she had only realized the level of difficulty to which she had elevated this situation for the ones she loved so much.

I remember thinking to myself, "Felicia, why did you feel so desperate that you believed taking your life was the best option?" I remember distinctly being very, very angry with her. I was becoming emotionally involved in this call, and I found that my personal reaction would later affect many aspects of my future in police work.

I was really moved by this situation, and I was continually being overwhelmed with each note I saw, with each provision she had made, and with each glance at her distraught ex-husband (with whom Felicia still obviously had a very amiable and loving relationship). As if all of this were not enough, hanging up on a hanger right next to the set of letters was an incredibly beautiful dress. Felicia had pinned a note to this dress, stating that she wanted to be buried in it. I remember thinking to myself, "This woman has a brain tumor and was facing a surgery. She must have been so desperate. Look at all she has done to prepare for the end of her existence here on earth. I wish I had been given the opportunity to know this woman." I was sad, emotionally drained, and it had been a long day. By the time we finally got to leave the scene, it was nearly 1:00 a.m.

I had not been out on the streets long enough to know how to deal with this type of call on a personal level. I went home and got ready for bed. Before trying to sleep, I fell prostrate on the floor of my apartment. I began wailing with grief, as I was finally able to release all of the emotions I had been forced to hold in all night. I will never forget praying, begging, even yelling at God.

"Why did you let her do this?" "Why was this woman so desperate?" "Why did she have to die slowly? Were you punishing her?"

I cried out to the woman, as well, "Felicia! Why did you do this?" "Don't you see what you have done?"

I had to pray for a very long time, earnestly begging for God to remove what had become faulty thinking on my part. I had taken way too much ownership of this experience. I could not allow things to affect me like this. If I did, I would be completely useless as an officer; I would be unfit, and I would have to leave this career. I had overcome many personal struggles during the academy. I decided that I would have to consider this an incredibly potent learning experience, put it into perspective, and move on.

By allowing myself to grieve for this woman, and with guidance from God, I was able to let go of the situation. Even so, I have never forgotten about Felicia. Her decision to end her life that night allowed me to see into my own heart and mind. She had forced me to face some of my own demons - the demons that were causing me to doubt my suitability for this job. Again, with God's help, the demons were expelled from the picture. It would take me fifteen years to recognize a plan for me to use these experiences for more than just police work. These experiences equipped me with compassion and understanding that would be essential in my future field of counseling.

## Don't Mess with my Clerk!

Like the "'Minty-Fresh' Drunk" story above, even though the account in this story does not represent a suicide attempt, it still demonstrates the sheer desperation some people exhibit when they have a desire for a certain outcome. Sometimes these desires become overwhelming and are accompanied by a total disregard for the risks involved and the resulting consequences. It routinely appears that the anticipation of success far outweighs the possibility of failure in the criminal mind. This may be because the justice system often allows hardened criminals to re-enter society before they have been rehabilitated. Of course, it is also possible that some people just do not care about the potential consequences until they are looming before them. It is not clear which is the case with regards to the suspects in the following story.

For midnight shift officers, there are very few establishments that are open for business during the quiet overnight hours. Back in 1993, there were even fewer than there are today. As a result of working that shift, it became necessary to frequent such establishments as convenience stores and overnight restaurants and cafés to acquire refreshments such as drinks and snacks, and to use the facilities during the shift. These types of places were also essential for field officers to enter police reports. Back during that time, officers were required to call in offense and incident reports to a dictation system. This required access to a phone, preferably in a quiet place. The managers of convenience stores and 24-hour restaurants would graciously allow officers to use their desks and telephones for this purpose. This was the case because the presence of an officer's car, along with the knowledge that an officer was in their building for an extended period of time was rather comforting to the employees during the solitary, quiet hours of the night shift.

My particular "office" spot was the 7-Eleven located at the corner of Hemphill Street and Allen Avenue. There were several clerks who rotated shifts at this store, but one in particular was usually there while I was on duty. I will call him Ray. Ray was a really personable guy, and most of the officers in the area would come by and chat with him occasionally throughout the shift while getting a soda or completing paperwork. I developed a pretty strong bond with Ray because I would see him as much, if not more than I would see other officers during a busy shift. This was especially true for me because this store was in my assigned beat area at the time.

Most officers will tell you that at some point throughout a law-enforcement career he has pondered (or maybe even fantasized) about driving up on a robbery in progress and being able to apprehend the suspects while rescuing the employees and customers of the targeted establishment. Considering this truth, along with the fact that most officers had certain clerks and waitresses in the community who became dear to them for the reasons described above, it will be easy for you to understand why this story is pretty much a dream-come-true for any officer, much less a rookie officer as I was during the time of its occurrence.

One Friday night in February of 1993, I was working my normal shift and beat area when another officer and I had just completed a call. We were both headed to our 7-Eleven to do paperwork and make our routine pit-stop. As I was driving southbound down Hemphill Street, approaching the store, I noticed two males exiting the front doors hastily, looking around suspiciously as they ran. These two guys dashed around the building and behind it, disappearing into the darkness.

I immediately suspected a robbery had occurred. I was not sure if my partner, who was driving in a separate car behind me, had seen what I had. I got on the radio and called out to the dispatcher that we needed to initiate an investigation at 1600 Hemphill Street. I learned that my partner *had* seen the two guys, and he immediately veered off and chased after the two men. He pulled his vehicle behind the store and exited it, running on foot in pursuit. He was able to swiftly capture one of the two guys who had just left the store in haste, and place him into custody. I remained in my patrol vehicle and drove around from the other side of the store and kept the second male on view as he climbed an eight-foot fence. Little did he know that the fence he climbed was an abandoned enclosure which would keep him contained until other officers made the scene to secure him, as well.

I did not climb the fence because my partner was nearby with the first suspect, and I could see the second suspect clearly from where I was. He was tired, and was not going anywhere with my pistol pointed at him. My location outside the enclosure kept me available to my partner in case he had any problems while other officers were in route.

Every officer who worked that area knew that if the 7-Eleven was robbed, it would be a friend employed there who was the victim. By mere human nature this provoked a heightened sense of urgency for all of the responding officers. Before we knew it, there were about ten additional patrol officers present, several of whom had no problem scaling that fence and taking the second suspect into custody.

After both of the suspects were safely in custody, other officers relocated to the store to question our clerk about what had just happened. He was completely terrified, trembling from fear and adrenaline. Ray had been working behind the counter when the two males entered the store. One of the suspects yelled at Ray and said, "Open the drawer and get down or I will shoot you!" He made a gesture with his hand under his jacket, indicating that he was holding a pistol. After Ray opened the cash drawer on the register, one of the suspects went behind the counter and pushed him down onto the floor. Ray was terrified, believing he was about to be shot and killed.

A second clerk had emerged from the stock room and surprised the robbers. He was asked to get down, as well. He was completely clueless as he unknowingly walked out into the store and interrupted the robbery. He, too, was mortified as he obediently hit the floor in one of the aisles.

Every clerk must inevitably consider this scenario at some time during his or her career, praying that it never happens. Unfortunately, it is a reality which occurs entirely too often. Ray and his colleague remained down on the floor as the suspect continued to clean out the cash from the register while his partner began to collect cartons of cigarettes.

During this episode, the two men loaded up on cash and as many cartons of cigarettes as they could stuff into their clothing. All the time Ray and the other clerk were huddled down. One was lying down in the aisle - the other behind the counter, each fearing for his life. Eventually, both men had all the stolen goods they could carry in their jackets and arms, and they quickly left the scene. This is when, by the grace of God, my partner and I happened to be driving up to the store. Thankfully and miraculously, we were there at just the right time to capture both of these men who had just terrorized "our clerks."

Subsequently it was determined that neither of the men actually had a pistol. They were simply acting as if they did. Even so, no clerk ever wants to gamble and find out whether a robber is bluffing or not.

Furthermore, it was discovered that each one of these suspects was out on parole, having just been released from prison for previous robberies. On this night, each of the men would be charged with yet another, which would be upgraded to "aggravated robbery" because of the threat made with the gesture of the pistol. We hoped that perhaps this time their actions would result in a more serious penalty. These two obviously needed to be in prison for a considerable amount of time for the consequence to hit home for them. Whatever the case, they would not be victimizing our 7-Eleven employees again for awhile. We were able to return the cash and the cigarettes to the store after processing them as evidence. It was nice, for once, to be able to recover something for a victim.

At the time of this robbery, I had only been "cut-loose" for four months. Our Sergeant wrote commendations for the officers who were involved, which was rather satisfying for me, especially so early in my career. This is, without a doubt, one of the most remarkable memories of my fifteen years, not only because we were able to drive up in the nick of time to foil an aggravated robbery, but more so because the victims were some of our very dear friends who did not deserve such terror as they tried to earn a decent living by working a real job.

# Chapter Ten
## Breaking the Rules – (The Statute of Limitations Has Passed)
*[These stories contain unprofessional behavior, ignorance and immaturity]*

### Donut Excursion

Any time someone wants to address a police officer with a wise-crack, it usually involves some type of sarcastic comment about "eating donuts." While I must admit that I enjoy a nice glazed one every once in a while, I have never experienced withdrawals if I failed to stop and grab a daily dozen crème filled or crullers at the local donut shop. Even so, the moment a civilian catches an officer eating a donut, that officer is toast. Actually, I rarely, if ever, desired a donut, and especially not while I was on duty. That is, until they began dotting the Metroplex with "Krispy Kreme" donut shops. Those donuts are enchanting. They have some secret ingredient in them that draws me to them, like Wimpy's nose following the irresistible scent that leads to a delicious hamburger in the classic Popeye cartoons.

While I worked for the School Security Initiative, officers in that unit were assigned to a particular school. We were to remain on the campus during the school day, every day, for the entire school year. An officer was stationed in each of the high schools and middle schools within the city limits of Fort Worth. Our duty was to maintain order and be available to address emergency situations should anything happen that might pose a danger for the students or staff members. I was assigned to this unit for the last nine years of my career, and in the course of that tour of duty, I was assigned to several different schools. However, I spent the most years as the School Resource Officer for an alternative ninth grade campus on the south side of the city. One of my fellow officers (and very close friend) was assigned to a middle school nearby, and as a result, when the need would arise, we would be able to assist one another. We were also able to take our breaks together.

During the summer months when school was out, we were often assigned to patrol the areas near our schools and perform routine checks of registered sex-offenders. This basically involved acquiring the list of registered sex-offenders for our area and making home visits to ensure compliance to the requirements of his or her court ordered registration. During this time, it was always wise to have a partner along for safety purposes. As a result, my friend and I decided to work together at this task. This was especially logical because our schools were so close together, and our offender lists often overlapped.

After a morning of waking up angry people and trying to ascertain that their papers were in order, we started thinking of what we might eat for lunch. On this particular day, we both thought of how wonderful it would be to just eat an entire box of Krispy Kreme donuts. We were both hungry, and those glazed, hot, flaky donuts sounded so tempting! Unfortunately, however, at the time, the franchise was just beginning to emerge in the Metroplex. There were no locations in Fort Worth. The only location within twenty miles was the one on Cooper Street in Arlington.

Now I have never been one to blatantly break the rules, especially at work. As a matter of fact, I have always had a reputation for following the rules. That's why it seemed a bit surprising to those around me when I confessed this story. Shamefully, I admit that I did it. I actually drove my patrol vehicle to Arlington, on duty, to get Krispy Kreme donuts. However, I didn't do it alone! My friend (who will remain nameless) and I decided that we would make it an adventure to get some of those fresh hot glazed donuts, even though it would involve quite a risky trek into another city! After all, we were allotted a forty-five minute lunch break (but we were not expected to drive forty-five miles during it to get to our food). This was so against the rules that it still makes me nervous thinking about it today.

Even so, we began our approximately twenty-mile-each-way trip that would lead us far out of our authorized area and into another jurisdiction. I don't know why we did this. I really don't. However, we did, and as we drove there, I became more and more nervous as I approached the city limits that segued from Fort Worth into Arlington. We drove through heavy traffic onto Cooper Street, and moved closer and closer to the subject of our impromptu obsession. I could see the beautiful green, red and white sign perched proudly in front of the donut shop up ahead.

Suddenly, however, I had the most overwhelming feeling of panic. I began to shake, and my heart began racing. I started thinking of things that could happen that would get us caught. I knew that at any moment we could be involved in a traffic accident. Someone could run a red light, swerve over into our lane, run into the back of the car as we were stopped at an intersection, or any number of other traffic mishaps that arbitrarily happen countless times each day. Then I began thinking about the possibility of one of our tires going flat. We did not carry spares. We were contracted to call for a tire truck in the event of a flat – but not from Arlington. After that, I began thinking of citizens who might try to flag us down for assistance. What if someone were robbing the bank we were passing by, right now? What if someone spotted his stolen car right in front of us, and needed our help? A million "what if" scenarios began racing through my mind.

I told my friend I was getting scared, and the feeling was mutual. Even so, we could see the sign up ahead. We had made it almost halfway through this shameful excursion, and there could be no turning back now without eternal regret. We pulled up into the drive-through lane to order our donuts. I was afraid to turn the car off and go inside for fear that it might not start back up again. I had experienced no problems with the car, but I knew that "Murphy's Law of Trekking Out of Authorized Area to Purchase Krispy Kreme Donuts" dictated that if you turn of the engine of the Fort Worth patrol vehicle in Arlington, the car would not start again.

We ordered a dozen plain glazed donuts in the drive through. We travelled all that way and risked so much trouble for six donuts each. For a short moment, all of my inhibitions left me as the young man at the window handed over one of those famous white-and-green spotted boxes full of heavenly aromatic donuts into my possession. I paid for them, and as I edged out of the drive through, reality set in with me, once again. Now that we had these donuts, we had to get back to Fort Worth without any of the travesties I had feared actually happening to us.

I pulled over to the side of the parking lot for just a moment, and took out one of those perfectly delectable hot donut creations from the box. Then my partner and I both enjoyed the first of many glorious bites of Krispy Kreme bliss. I must say, however, before my first bite I thanked God for it, and then I promptly made a silent, but earnest plea for mercy. I sincerely begged Him that He might allow us to make it back into the city before getting involved in any type of mishap that could get us disciplined or fired. I made a silent bargain with God. I promised that although this was the first time I had ever made such ignorant decision that could place my job and reputation in jeopardy, it would also be my last, whether we made it back safely or not.

I took a deep breath and entered the roadway, carefully, heading back south on Cooper Street towards Interstate 20. If I could just get on the freeway, I would feel much better. However, traffic was getting heavier and heavier, because it was the lunch rush hour in this very busy city. We sat through several cycles of each traffic light, stuck in the forever stretching line of cars rushing around trying to get to and from the responsibilities of their day.

All I could do was to pray constantly that none of these people would hit my car. As we sat there in the traffic, we both became very nervous about the situation we had put ourselves in. Each one of us ate donut after donut, until we had only a few left in the box that had originally held a full dozen. Finally, by the grace of God, we made it onto the freeway. Now it was time for a celebration donut, so we each had another. This diminished our stash down to just a couple of lonely donuts left sitting in the box. They were so good when they were fresh and hot – why not? We each grabbed one of the last two donuts in the box as I drove west down the freeway, just miles now from the Fort Worth City Limits. As we passed over the borderline safely, we each finished the last bite of our six donuts each. An amazing feeling of victory surged through our veins as we were once again in the safe City of Fort Worth. We were still out of our authorized area, but at least now if we had a mishap of some sort, we were in the right city!

We made it all the way back to our neighborhood and commenced our work. After we were back in our area, in the safe place where we knew we would not be caught, we began to laugh uncontrollably. We had eaten an entire dozen donuts just driving back to the city. I felt a rush of excitement and relief from having survived that entire ordeal. Most likely the rush was from excessive amounts of sugar. Let it be noted, however, that I kept my promise to God and I never did a bonehead thing like that again. It would definitely not be worth the stress!

*There has been a long-standing myth that police officers must consume donuts and coffee in order to function, although there is no concrete evidence to support this assertion - or is there? In this photo: Steve Martin*

## Coffin Caper

Occasionally on midnight shift patrol officers experience periods of time where things are actually quiet in the city. It was during these times that we would take the initiative to check on businesses in the area, making sure that they were secured. One such slow night, while I was riding with another officer, we received a message on our Mobil Data Terminal (MDT) summonsing us to meet with another couple of units near the intersection of Rosedale Street and Evans Avenue. Upon our arrival, my partner and I listened as another officer told us about finding

113

an abandoned funeral home nearby. The officer had discovered that the funeral home had an unsecured open door. He did not want to search this building alone, especially in light of the type of establishment it was. After all, this place had been abandoned for at least ten years, and it was creepy! Recognizing the unlikelihood of anyone being inside this place due to its sheer nature, and further realizing that there was probably nothing of value inside that anyone would care to steal, we agreed to assist in this building search admittedly more out of the desire for an adventure than from a sense of duty.

We all changed locations and approached the dark, quiet, and creepy abandoned funeral home. It was about 3:00 a.m. and there was not much of anything moving in the neighborhood. As we pushed open the unlocked door and began to walk inside, it creaked with a spine-chilling squeak, just like in the dramatics of a corny scary movie. It was not uncommon for any of us to search a dark, abandoned building in the middle of the night, but this place was different.

Usually we expected to perhaps find a suspect hiding in the dark. Here, we did not expect that; as a matter of fact, we did not know what to expect. We moved from room to room in pairs, inspecting the premises. There was a business office, a chapel, a room full of coffins that had been on display, and a surgical room where corpses were prepared for viewing. Everything we saw was being illuminated by the light of our flashlights, alone. As the lights moved around from room to room, eerie shadows appeared and all of us became a bit spooked by the sheer creepiness of this place. It was the classic example of a ghostly, macabre mortuary.

In one large room there were metal gurneys on wheels, cabinets filled with antique looking medical implements including sharp needles and cutting instruments. There was a large double sink nearby, and a concrete floor covered with little white square tiles that angled downward towards a large metal drain in the middle of the floor. Who knows how many gallons of blood and body fluids had been washed down that drain? We were all a bit on edge, because we were really surprised to find this prep room still intact. Although the funeral home had been abandoned for quite some time, it had been preserved in pristine fashion and still appeared to be ready for business. The appointment book in the office was opened to a date in the early 1980's, and this was some time in the middle 1990's. The creepiness was indescribable.

Once it was determined that we were the only four people in this place, the mischievous nature began to kick in with some of my colleagues. An officer from one of the other units quietly asked me to lure one of the other officers into a different section of the building while the other two stayed behind. He asked me to stall for a couple of minutes, and then come back to the same room – the room where the coffins were being displayed. I complied with this request, knowing what they had in mind. We walked through the chapel area, talking about scary movies we had seen where the holy water jumps around and splashes when someone enters the sanctuary alone in the dark.

We had talked ourselves into a fright when I said, "Let's go back and see what the others are doing, and let's get out of here!" My partner agreed with this plan, and we maneuvered back towards the coffin display room.

The other officer met us. He said, "As soon as we find my partner, we can go. Have you seen him?"

Of course the answer was "No."

The other officer began to call his partner's name, and about that time we heard a slow creaking sound coming from the coffin directly in front of us. It was beginning to open. Suddenly the top flew up on it quickly, and the fourth officer sat up inside it and yelled loudly. My partner saw this and literally fell backward, almost fainting from surprise and sheer terror. Once he realized that it was one of his fellow officers, he got really angry for a moment, and then we all laughed until we could hardly stand up anymore. After that little bit of fun, we respectfully made certain that everything was returned to the state in which we found it, and we left, pulling the door closed, with a click of the lock.

## I'm In Charge!

As representatives of our city, Fort Worth Officers are expected to uphold the highest standards of courtesy and service to our citizens at all times. I have always ascribed to this philosophy. That is, with a few exceptions. Here is one of them.

It was the Fourth of July holiday and I was working traffic control at one of the worst intersections in the city after the fireworks display. I knew this meant heavy traffic, horns honking, people cursing at me, and the like. I was prepared for that. I was fine with it, as a matter of fact, until the sheer numbers of impatient people in the cars began to develop a mob mentality. It was then that I lost my ability to "let it slide."

I was assigned to the intersection of White Settlement Road and Calvert Street, which is just north of downtown. This was known as the prime viewing area for the fireworks that were set off on the Trinity River bank nearby. As a result of its proximity to the main stage, this intersection was bursting with cars from every direction, because there had been literally thousands of cars packed into every nook and cranny possible along the river.

Cars were parked on the grass, the sidewalks, up on medians, and there weren't enough police in America to keep them out of these places during the area-renowned Fort Worth fireworks display. When the cars started pouring in at the beginning of the evening, everyone had a reason why he should be allowed to park in restricted areas. They would produce credentials in every form one could imagine, or "name-drop" some prominent figure who "told them they could park there because..."

I would continuously hear, "My husband is so and so..." or, "I own this business right down here..." "But officer, you don't realize who I am..." and the list goes on. These "special" people began to fill up the areas that weren't designed for traffic flow. I thought, "If they want to be there that bad, they can be there. I certainly can't stop them, and no one else is."

However, they did have to leave eventually, and this is when every "special" carload of people expected a police escort from the riverbed to the freeway.

When the fireworks show ended, I was already aggravated by the fact that the police were simply outnumbered and unable to enforce minor traffic violations that were becoming overbearing in such numbers. My job was to clear out the traffic from the hundreds of driveways, sidewalks, medians and parking lots, in an attempt to maintain some type of order. The term "gridlock" does not do justice to describe the situation that night. Even so, I began to methodically cycle cars through, taking turns from every direction, just as I had been trained to do.

Apparently during one cycle of this traffic flow my judgment did not meet the approval of some of the drivers. I had not allowed enough cars to pass through the intersection during the previous cycle, according to the people in the first two vehicles, who were now waiting their turn in the line. They began honking their horns immediately. Horns were sounding everywhere, so this was not particularly creative. These same spectators in the first and second vehicle began cursing at me. I was not impressed by that, either. However, when the honking and the cursing didn't elicit a response from me, the driver of the second car catapulted an empty glass beer bottle out his window at me. It shattered in the street, just feet from where I was standing. Incidentally, because it was about 98 degrees outside I was wearing the approved police uniform shorts, which did not go well with shards of glass bouncing off the pavement.

I became enraged. I was one person in the middle of the intersection surrounded by what seemed like thousands of impatient, angry, and drunk drivers. I had no recourse whatsoever for anyone who failed to follow my directives. I could not leave my post to address the man who threw the bottle at me. There were no other officers around to assist me. I was on the verge of losing control of the situation. Even so, I kept telling myself, "I am in charge, here!"

I allowed the other three lines to move through the normal cycle during their turns. When it was time for the fourth line of cars (the troublemakers), I turned to them, made eye-contact with the driver of the first car (which is the only one who matters) and held my hand up in the "stop" position. I smirked and giggled inside as I passed over them and returned to the first line and cycled through the entire intersection, again. This made the guys in those first two cars livid. The driver of the second car who had thrown the bottle at me exited his car and began walking out into the intersection towards me. I welcomed him. I would have loved to have cuffed him and left him to lie on the hot pavement, in broken glass, as the cars drove by within a foot of his head. However, I somehow snapped back into the mindset where judgment existed.

I warned the man by pointing down to the field of amber colored glass shards all around me. "This broken bottle is why you and everyone else in this line are not moving. If you ever want to get through this intersection tonight, I suggest you get back into your car and refrain from throwing any more items. If you don't get back into your car, I will take you to jail."

The man kept walking towards me, still yelling and cursing. Suddenly the people in the other cars realized that *he* was their problem, and not me. They started yelling and cursing at him, telling him to get back into the car. After a heated exchange between this man and the other drivers, he realized that *he* was now facing the angry mob. He also had what looked like a couple of hundred cars backed up behind him on White Settlement Road that were going to be following him out of there, going the same direction he was. He finally got the picture, and returned to his car.

I finished the cycles of the intersection, and when it was time for them to go, this time, I let them. I allowed that line to go for a substantially longer time than the normal cycle, because some innocent people were undoubtedly stuck in the mayhem behind these two losers. Later I realized that my behavior had been congruent with that of the drunks, in that it lacked maturity. I responded to the stress and overwhelming pressure of having been in an unpleasant situation by reacting like a child. This was one of the times in my life when I completely ignored that still, small voice inside of me that prodded me to "Love thy neighbor as thy self."

Instead of loving those obnoxious drunks, I became angry, played their game, and acted childish. Even so, I must admit that, at the time, I took great pleasure in doing so. When these drivers got nasty with me, I showed them who was in charge. Eventually, the rest of the mob showed them, too! My lack of professionalism aside, this was one of the best instances of positive peer pressure I had ever seen. Although I taught myself an important lesson about self-control, after all was said and done, my actions seemed to have worked like a charm.

## Taxi Ride to Nowhere

This is one of those types of stories where someone could undoubtedly get into trouble if the incident had not happened so long ago. Thankfully, it has been at least fourteen years, and I feel quite confident that the likelihood of any repercussions is improbable. However, if an officer did this today, he or she would probably get disciplined heartily. Even so, when my partner and I did this, we were actually directed to do it by a supervisor – and that always helps.

The south side area has always had more than a fair share of transients who stand on the corners and medians loitering and begging. One particularly busy location for this was the intersection of Rosedale and I-35. This corner had a pair of men who would come out, often late at night and stand with signs, asking for money. They eventually developed a ploy where one would distract the driver, and the other would open the passenger-side door and steal the driver's purse. Sometimes this pair would use a weapon and actually rob drivers who were stopped at the light. As a result of these robberies, my partner and I hit that corner regularly and issued citations to document every person we could as they badgered the poor, innocent drivers on Rosedale.

As we were monitoring this intersection over the course of several days, we recognized that one man in particular, who I will call Rodney, was at the intersection every day and every night, and would never even attempt to comply with our orders to vacate the area. He would even taunt us because he did not care about receiving a citation. He was homeless, and he realized that after awhile his citations would turn to warrants, and he would be given a free ride to the jail. This was great. It brought him the opportunity for three square meals, a shower, and a place to sleep for a few days while he "sat out" his citation fees.

Rodney quickly became one of our least favorite persons on the south side. Every officer knew him, and every officer issued citations to him. He was fresh out of jail from sitting out some of the fees from recent warrants. As a result, he knew it would be awhile before he was able to go back. He cheerfully welcomed the regular visits with the officers, and made a game out of these contacts by mocking, snickering, and taunting them. He knew that our hands were tied, and we had no other recourse but to continue what we had been doing – issuing tickets. Often when we would hand him his copy of the citation, he would pull out a stack of folded papers from his pocket and snicker as he methodically arranged the newest one on the top of the stack. He had no scruples whatsoever.

One night, after we had just seen Rodney and had issued him his nightly ticket, he returned back to the street almost immediately afterward. My partner and I became so aggravated by this blatant disrespect from this heinous man that we contacted a supervisor. We spoke with him by phone and asked permission to take creative action. Believe it or not, our supervisor liked our idea, and gave us his blessing, even though it involved breaking about three or four of our policies.

We returned to the corner and approached Rodney. As per routine, he appeared happy to see us. He never avoided our directives to step over to our car. On this night, however, when Rodney came over to us, we exited the vehicle and quickly cuffed him. He snickered and said, "I don't have any warrants – I just got out a few days ago, but if you want to take me to jail, please do. I need a shower!" We placed Rodney in the car after patting him down.

My partner and I laughed with an evil snicker. We weren't headed to jail. We weren't headed anywhere close, as a matter of fact. Our destination would be a mystery as we drove away from this familiar corner. We entered the freeway service road to I-35 and headed north. Rodney thought we were headed downtown, even though it would have been the longest route to jail. He did not show much concern. However, when we passed the exits to downtown, he began to ask questions. "Hey! Where are you taking me?"

"You'll see" was our reply. Our faces both had mile-wide grins. Rodney was getting nervous. "What are you doing?" He asked. We just ignored him, kept smiling, and kept driving.

It was 1994, and development in north Fort Worth did not extend much past the Summerfields neighborhood and Western Center Blvd. Today, however, development extends almost to the Oklahoma border. At the time, we knew that it would be rather difficult for Rodney to panhandle on I-35 in rural Denton County. As a result, we were headed to the Denton County line. That was our destination. We kept travelling north for another fifteen miles or so, and the bright lights of the City began to dim, getting further and further behind us. Eventually, the existence of the occasional roadside convenience stores began to dwindle. Things became eerily desolate and dark. Finally, up ahead was that big green sign that said, "Denton County."

This is where we exited the freeway. Rodney's snide remarks, snickering and taunting had been replaced with a genuine fear. He displayed the first look of concern we had ever seen on his face. It was unusual to see Rodney shaken up and he appeared to be somewhat worried and afraid. Quite honestly, I must admit, we relished the thought with much pleasure. It was wrong, I know, but we were so tired of this man's menacing contribution to our beat area on the south side of town that we were just simply fed-up.

"What are you going to do to me?" He asked.

"Absolutely nothing," was our reply.

He was perplexed, and we were experiencing way too much satisfaction from his nervous demeanor. We stopped the car at a dark overpass. There was no convenience store, no street light, and no restaurant for miles. We could barely see the yellow lights from a blinking traffic warning light a mile or so further north from where we had stopped. This was the perfect place.

We got out of the car and opened the back passenger door. Rodney did not want to get out of the car. He thought we were going to kill him and leave him out in the middle of nowhere. He was only halfway right. We pulled him out of the car as he struggled to stay in, like a frightened cat hiding under the bed, fearing for his life. When he was finally coaxed out, he asked in a begging tone, "You aren't going to kill me are you?"

"Of course not! We are not going to hurt you at all. We are going to let you go, right here!" Rodney's demeanor shifted from fear, to relief, to extreme anger within seconds. We removed his cuffs and told him, "Goodnight."

He began to curse at us. "You guys can't do this to me!" I will have you fired! We thought, "Okay. Go ahead and try." We knew we were safe. After all, our supervisor had given us permission and directed us to take him to the Denton County line. We were only following orders. Besides that, Rodney had a reputation with our Department as having been a high-level nuisance. We weren't worried about his threats.

We entered the vehicle again and sped off onto the overpass, heading back south. We were both laughing like little kids who had pulled a really remarkable prank. At least, for tonight, the intersection of Rosedale and I-35 would be free of Rodney. We knew he would find his way back, probably by the next day. Even so, we enjoyed the satisfaction of having rocked this guy's world for the night. We had finally been able to find a way to inconvenience him, and even instilled a bit of fear into his soul. It was sweet success. Thankfully, as we drove away, it was too dark for us to see the obscene gesture that Rodney was throwing up in our honor.

## Parking Ticket Assistant

It was not uncommon for supervisors to assign a ride-in to share a shift with me when I worked the midnight shift. I did not mind having someone along who wanted to learn about police work. On those nights when I had my eager visitors, I took great care to explain the policies and safety precautions in order to keep them safe while providing them with the most fun and excitement possible. One night, however, I invited my cousin to ride along with me. She had expressed the desire to become an officer, and was curious about what the career actually entailed. I guess because I knew her well and felt comfortable with her I must have treated her with a little less consideration. If she wanted to know what police work was like, I would show her – no holds barred.

Despite my desire to please her thirst for crime-fighting excitement, this was a relatively slow night. Actually, it was really quiet and boring. I needed to find something creative to do to pique the interest of my guest. At roll call that night, we had been notified of some parking complaints in a neighborhood on my beat. As a result, I decided to take my ride-in out for the experience of citing parking violations. Because it was much easier to do with a partner, I decided that I would enlist her assistance with the task. Once we arrived, I pointed out the violations which were truly excessive in this area.

The citizen who had complained had a valid point. The street looked like a junkyard. There were cars sitting on blocks in obvious disrepair. Some were on the road with several flat tires, while some were parked in yards without improved driveways, and still others were parked on the wrong side of the road at an angle. All of these were violations, and I realized that I would be issuing several citations on this street. I began to write them out, one-by-one, as I sat in the car. I told my cousin (who if you will remember had expressed a desire to become an officer) that it would be her job to place the citations underneath the windshield wipers of the violating vehicles. She looked at me with shock and near disbelief. She thought I was kidding. I reminded her that she wanted to do this job, and this was a part of it!

I continued to complete the citations for two or three cars at a time that were within close proximity to one another. I would hand them to my cousin and send her running for her life as she rushed to deliver them to each car before someone heard us and peeked out a window or opened a door. She moved quickly, in a race against time and the unknown. She was scared to death that someone would open the door and confront her about her being around their vehicle. I laughed as she expressed her displeasure with this task. "Are you trying to get me killed?" she asked me, out of breath from running to and from the violating cars.

I warned her that if anyone came to the door of the house she was to simply run and jump into the patrol car where she would be safe. She thought I was out of my mind. After several trips to cars and back, she was done. Apparently, the fear of being shot by an angry resident was beginning to take its toll on her. I laughed at her and reminded her that she had asked for excitement. When there was nothing going on, I figured this was my best bet for making some fun for her. I never would have placed her in danger, but if something had happened, I would have probably had some explaining to do as to why my ride-along had been shot at while placing a parking ticket on a junked car in a front yard.

## Torturing Teenagers

One summer night shift when I was patrolling the south side beat that extends to the area just east of the Fort Worth Zoo, my partner and I had been working calls together from separate patrol vehicles. We decided to go to the parking lot at the Forest Park community swimming pool and catch up on some paperwork. When we arrived, however, we got quite a surprise as we saw a group of several teenagers, males and females, swimming in the pool. It was about 2:00 a.m. and besides the fact that they were trespassing, it wouldn't have been such a big deal, except for one thing. They were naked. That's right; these kids were out there in the community pool swimming in the nude. The overhead lighting was on, and the pool was clearly lit. In the midst of the sparkling clear blue water was a cluster of naked bodies. When they saw the two patrol vehicles pull up into the lot, they got out of the water and began running towards the darkness, and the cover of the woods, looking for a place to hide. I saw more full moons that night than you could find in an old horror movie convention. A couple of the young ladies were wearing underwear, but most of the rest of these kids were completely naked.

We pulled up and approached the area to check out the situation. To our delight, there was a pile of clothing sitting on the edge of the pool. My male colleague, like me, had a sinister side, and we both began thinking of ways to make these kids' lives miserable. We knew they were "stuck" with nowhere to go without their clothes. As any understanding adult would do upon finding teenagers in such a pinch, we grabbed up the clothing and took it back to our patrol vehicle. Then, after we locked the car, we approached the fenced in area again. We called out to the group, who was hiding behind the pool house. We could hear the crunching of leaves and twigs, and an occasional whisper. Finally, out of the sheer realization that they had no other choice, one of the male teens called back out to us from his cover in the darkness.

"We are back here, officers. We need our clothes!"

We were trying with all of our might not to burst into laughter, because we knew these kids could see us, even though we couldn't see them. We didn't want to laugh at them, at least not yet, not in front of their faces. My partner made a deal with the young man from which the voice emanated out of the dark woods behind the pool house. He would give this young man his clothing, and this kid would give the others their clothing. There was a catch. Each one of them would have to get dressed and come to talk with us face to face. If anyone ran, the others would all be cited for trespassing.

After each of the kids got their clothing and got dressed, they were forced to come out of the darkness and face the embarrassment of talking to both of us officers. They had to give us their names and other identifying information so we could document their having been there. We decided to give each one of them a warning instead of a citation, but they were still mortified at having to come out from behind the building and meet with us.

We explained to them that they were not to come back to the pool after hours. The next time they would receive the trespassing citations, and maybe even the disorderly conduct – exposure citations for being naked. These young people were very accommodating and grateful for the leniency, even though they were very clearly humiliated. It was easy to give them a break, but hard not to laugh. After all, could you imagine being in their shoes? Actually, I should say, could you imagine not being in their shoes, *or their shorts, or their shirts*? I'm sure everyone has been in a situation at some time in his or her life where vulnerability prevailed. During these times, discretion and mercy is merited – maybe due to nothing more than simple human compassion. We remembered what it was like to be a teenager. They were taking a risk, being daring, and trying to have a little innocent fun. After all, skinny-dipping is far better than what most teenagers today do for fun. All in all, we gave them enough trouble to deter future attempts at naked-night swimming, but we weren't merciless. Even so, when they were all gone, we were finally able to laugh – and that we did that without the least bit of mercy.

# Chapter Eleven
## New Year's Eve

### Under Cover – Literally!

Working as a police officer in a large city, one quickly learns that on certain holidays it is futile to attempt to conquer the ignorance of the masses. My midnight shift training officer, who became one of my favorite partners after training, taught me lessons far beyond the ones I learned during my training phases. For instance, on New Year's Eve midnight shift we were working calls together, and about ten minutes before midnight he sent me a message, "Follow me." I did not have any idea where he might have been headed, but I had learned a long time ago not to question him. He was an expert and I respected his status as such. I followed as he made his way to a railroad underpass near Main Street and Berry Street.

He pulled up underneath the bridge and backed up onto the concrete median. I pulled up next to him. His advice to me was this: "For the next twenty minutes, this is where we stay. It doesn't matter if we are dispatched to a robbery, a stabbing, or a major car crash – this is where we stay. It is self-preservation." Before I knew it, as we sat there under that massively thick concrete bridge, the echoes of gunfire began to sporadically sound throughout the area. Within moments, the sporadic sounds became a constant, deafening, barrage as residents in the community around us unloaded boxes of ammo straight up into the air. Although warnings had been broadcast in the media that the practice was extremely dangerous, illegal and stupid, these people valued the celebratory nature of gunfire over safety and adherence to the law.

Thanks to the wise counsel of my colleague, we were safely sheltered from the fallout. It was amazing to hear the constant spray of deafening gunfire that went on for about ten to fifteen minutes without a break in action. These people were insane! There was no way we could feasibly address the issue that was obviously occurring en mass. It was one of the few times where, as an officer, we had to face the reality that we were outnumbered, and self-preservation became paramount. During this time all we could really do was pray no innocent citizens would be hit by falling shrapnel.

My colleague prompted me to check out the "calls holding" screen on the computer in my car. There were overwhelming numbers of "shots fired" calls being reported. During the ten minutes we sat there, calls began piling up and their numbers quickly exceeded a hundred. Normally, on a really busy weekend or holiday night there might have been fifteen or twenty different types of calls queued into the system. I had never seen over a hundred, and especially not a hundred of the same type of call. It was unreal. Even so, and despite the dispatcher having sent us on one of those shots fired calls, we remained under cover until the constant popping dwindled to an occasional piercing crackle in the night.

The whole situation reminded me of preparing popcorn in a microwave. When it began, the sound of the popping was constant and vigorous, overlapping for several minutes. Then, eventually, the pops became less frequent, until things seemed to become quiet again. Just when it appeared that it was all over, a lone pop would shatter the quiet, much like that one foreign kernel that waits until the very last possible moment to blossom into popcorn.

Much to my dismay, when this popcorn was done, we weren't able to enjoy a hot and buttery treat. Instead, I had to snap out of it and trudge into the nearby neighborhood in an attempt to find any of those citizens who had lingered outside with a celebratory pistol. Anyone we could catch would be dealt with harshly, but finding them was going to be nearly impossible. It took several hours for our team of officers who was working that night to knock out all of those calls, and almost no one actually caught a perpetrator who had been shooting. I imagine those other officers were also underneath their favorite bridge, dreaming about popcorn, too.

# On the Roof

Another New Year's Eve midnight shift when I was temporarily assigned to patrol, I was riding with a great friend of mine who worked in the School Security Initiative Unit with me. During the holidays, when school was out, the Department would routinely assign us to supplement patrol during busy times. As a result, we were out on the west side of Fort Worth during the reign of terror that was New Year's Eve. We were doing a special detail which involved being visible in the area in attempt to deter drunken driving, fireworks, and gunshots during the anticipated holiday revelry.

Midnight was drawing near, and having remembered the invaluable lesson that my previous colleague had taught me, I suggested a nice covered carport that we had found earlier in the shift. It was attached to a business on our assigned beat. Neither of us was very familiar with anything better in the neighborhood where we were working, so this carport would have to serve as sufficient cover for us. The most comforting aspect was the fact that it was a couple of blocks from the residential area, and homes were normally where the gunshots came from.

We were safely parked in our spot, planning to wait out the firefight. We were talking about the events of our day when the shooting began. It was a carbon copy of the event that happens every single year. Despite the urgent pleadings of authorities throughout media outlets, citizens will not refrain from firing celebratory shots indiscriminately into the air. As we listened, the deafening shots began.

This time, we were definitely prepared, though. We had made an early pit stop at a local convenience store and stocked up on snacks and drinks. We then sat in the patrol car and shared a chocolate Toblerone candy bar and let the surrounding members of the community empty their pistols to their hearts' content all around us. It didn't seem to bother us much, at all, considering that we were equipped with chocolate, soda and a carport.

During that crazy time while the gunshots were going off we received a dreaded call. Surprisingly enough, it wasn't a "shots fired" call. Instead it was a "possible burglary in progress" call. The details said that a group of kids was up on top of the roof at a nearby elementary school and it was unknown if they were trying to break in. We both laughed when we read the call screen. It seemed so ironic that we were strategically hiding under cover of a carport to avoid certain death and these ignorant kids were a few blocks away from us, right in the middle of the residential neighborhood, parading around on the rooftop of a school.

It was then that I remembered the second lesson from my former training officer: "Wait it out." We waited until the shots diminished to a dull roar, and then we reluctantly made our way to the school. While we were in route to the call, it began to rain. As cold as it was, we were almost certain that no one in his or her right mind would be hanging out on top of a roof for long under those conditions. Upon our arrival, we searched the entire area, and did not locate anyone up on top of the school roof that we could see from our vantage point. Our shift was almost over, and we were quite ready to try to beat the rush of traffic that would be filled with drunks sliding around on the wet roadways. After all, we would have to travel across the city to get to our own homes. As a result, we decided not to climb up on top of the roof and look for any kids. If there were an actual break-in, the alarm would have sounded. There was no alarm, so we figured it was just a group of kids being knuckleheads. The Air One police helicopter was grounded because of the relentless gunfire throughout the city. We both laughed as we wondered if there was a group of teenagers laid out up there on the roof, wounded or dead from gunshot fallout. Fortunately for us over the next few days there were no "missing persons" or "kids found shot on the roof" headlines in the local paper.

## Born on a Bridge

Finally, one of my most memorable New Year's Eve shifts was also very early in my career. I knew about the "take cover" philosophy, but on this night, Mother Nature had other plans. It was below freezing all during the shift, and the weather was threatening precipitation. In Texas, frozen rain, sleet, or snow on the roads is bad enough. No one knows how to drive in it, including yours truly. However, it is exponentially catastrophic on a night when the highest number of possible drunk drivers would be out on the roadways, travelling home from parties.

Around 12:30 a.m. it all began. People were winding down an enjoyable night of parties when the bottom fell out of the sky. A storm dropped massive amounts of sleet onto the roads. This literally could not have happened at a worse time. Although I have never been able to drive on icy roads, as an officer, I was out of luck with that excuse. It was my job to figure out how to maneuver through it, whatever that might entail. As a result, I was out in the middle of the mess, waiting for my assignment, ready to serve my city.

It wasn't long before I was sent out onto Interstate 20, westbound on the ramp that leads to southbound Interstate 35. By the grace of God I made it without crashing my car. My job here was to block off this access ramp. There was an accident way down the road on the ramp and a line of traffic was backed up there. I had to block the area for the safety of those trapped up on the bridge, and to give a buffer for those who were actually trying to back their way off of the bridge. It would be impossible for anyone to make it over the bridge, and extremely dangerous for anyone to attempt. As a result, several people were trying to retreat, which was a very tricky endeavor.

After spending over an hour helping to maneuver cars that were not involved in the accident as they attempted to back off of the slick bridge, I got word from a retreating driver that there was a medical emergency down in the middle of the pile of crashed cars on the entrance ramp. As it turned out, a woman had been on her way to the hospital in labor when the accident occurred. She was trapped in the midst of the crashed cars on the bridge. Unfortunately, there were no ambulances available, and although I kept checking on the police radio, my dispatcher continually advised me that all emergency response was busy and there was a very long wait for an ambulance. I felt desperate as I explained to her that there was a woman on the verge of giving birth on the bridge. Despite the fact that she needed medical assistance immediately, there was nothing we could do. While the dispatcher understood my predicament, as well as that of the woman in labor, the weather was so bad that there were just no ambulances available. The situation was made worse for me due to my inability to leave my post. As a result, it became clear that I could not have gotten to the woman, either, at least not before her newborn child was in kindergarten.

It took a couple of hours to get all of the cars off of the bridge. After a while I heard from another citizen that apparently somebody from the front side of the traffic jam on the bridge loaded the woman up in a passing vehicle and took her the rest of the way to the hospital. I never had the opportunity to check on her, because she was about a mile down the road from me on that icy bridge. It was confirmed that she was no longer on the scene when everything was cleared off of the bridge except the vehicle that she and her husband had been driving! They had to leave their car on the bridge and take that ride with a stranger to the hospital, so she could have her baby. All of this happened on New Year's Day, at about 1:00 a.m., in the sleet. I can only imagine that poor woman was dealing with one of the most miserable and stressful situations one could ever endure. I never heard how she made it through, and can only hope that everything was okay for the family. I also have never forgotten the desperation I felt being in a position where people were asking me for help, and I was not in a position to do anything for them except pray that everything would work out okay for them.

Overall, New Year's Eve was never one of my favorite times to work. There were always a ridiculous number of variables that tended to escalate the potential for normal problems to be exacerbated by drunks, weather, traffic, and gunfire. However adding emergency childbirth to the list of complications is a problem I definitely never expected!

# Chapter Twelve
## Traffic Turmoil

### "Make-Up" an Excuse

Most traffic violators do not enjoy interacting with the police when they are stopped. I have been stopped before, and I do not enjoy the feeling of wondering if I will be leaving the side of the road after having been put in my place with an expensive citation in tow. Even so, I have never been disrespectful to an officer because I fully recognize that he or she is just doing a very difficult job. Being on the other side of that phenomenon, however, it becomes clear that not everyone ascribes to the same philosophy as I do. As a matter of fact, some drivers can be just plain rude.

I worked the Traffic Unit on midnight shift for a couple of years, and while doing so, it was my job to address dangerous driving behaviors by stopping drivers and addressing the problem. I was assigned to the Driving While Intoxicated (D.W.I.) task force, and we were charged with the task of reducing traffic crashes caused by drunk drivers. In order to address this behavior, officers would stop vehicles that exhibited erratic driving behaviors including disregarding traffic laws or traffic control devices. Certain behaviors would indicate a higher likelihood of driver impairment, such as driving without lights at night, failing to maintain a lane, and hitting curbs. These violations were serious, because they placed other drivers in imminent danger. I never had a conscience problem stopping these drivers and placing them under arrest for their dangerous actions.

Make no mistake, however, in thinking that drunk drivers are the only dangerous drivers out on the road. Anyone who disregards speed limits or traffic control devices such as stop signs or lights contributes to the dangerous environment out on the roadways. Even worse, are instances of driver inattention, which can result in chaos when not accompanied by dumb luck. Consequently, officers assigned to the Traffic Division were expected to stop a high volume of vehicles and address these issues.

I never really enjoyed ruining people's day by writing them citations. Incidentally, I was always extremely fair about my decision to write a citation or not. I based my decision on a couple of objective factors. Either you had a driver's license and insurance, or you didn't. If I stopped a vehicle for running a stop sign or a red light, and the driver could present a driver's license and insurance, I would most likely send them on the way with a verbal warning. I believed that a citizen contact with a motorist could be a positive interaction with the police, and could ultimately boost citizen opinion of the Fort Worth Police Department. If citizens complied with the requirements each of us is expected to meet in order to earn the privilege of driving, there would not be a problem. However, if I asked for these items and the driver could not produce a license, insurance, registration and if they were not displaying an updated inspection sticker, I did not feel bad about issuing a ticket for the moving violation either.

I must have stopped a thousand cars during my career, and most of the time my experiences with drivers were unremarkable. However, from time to time I would get a hold of someone who had no understanding of driving safety. Some had a problem with authority, and others were just so wrapped up in their own little world that they had no concept that others were even alive around them. Some would be talking on the cell phone, others would have the stereo thumping, and yet others would be eating a full meal from his or her lap while I attempted to gather personal information for their ticket.

One afternoon while working a day shift assignment I watched in disbelief as a woman driving down Boat Club Road in far northwest Fort Worth was using her visor mirror to apply mascara. As she approached a curve in the roadway, her car went straight, and she cut off another vehicle in the lane next to her. I pulled her over and approached her. I have to admit I was a bit agitated with her unsafe driving. She only compounded this with her nonchalant attitude. Even so, I was courteous, and I asked for her license and insurance. I had made up my mind that this woman was leaving with a citation because her behavior was preposterous. She acted surprised when I grabbed her license and insurance card and told her I would be right back with her.

She leaned out her window and said, "Officer, are you writing me a ticket?"

I replied to her, "Yes, I will be just a moment."

She then became frustrated and said, "I have a date and I am running late to meet a guy I haven't seen since high school. I really need to go." I was in disbelief that she would tell me this, especially after she had just almost caused an accident by putting on her makeup while driving.

When I returned to the window to issue her ticket, she was angry. "You are making me late. I was already running late, and now I am really late." She dropped the name of an officer who was her friend. I was not impressed. I handed her the citation book to sign, and she grabbed it from me, angrily. This woman never understood why I wrote her a citation. In her eyes, I was being unreasonable and unfair. I was the obstacle keeping her from making it to her date on time. Never mind the fact that she almost caused a wreck, which would have inevitably propelled the mascara brush into her eyeball. I had actually probably saved this woman's eyesight. Even so, as is usually the case in these types of situations, she pegged me as the bad guy.

## Driving Barefoot

As most everyone does, I had days where I was not in the mood to tolerate bad attitudes from people. After all, I was doing my job, and I would not stop any driver unless I had a good reason. The reason always involved some violation of the law on their part. I stopped a man once who displayed an inspection sticker that had been expired for almost a year. When I approached him and asked for his other documents, he became irate with me. "Don't you have anything better to do?"

I calmly and courteously asked him again for his license and insurance. He flicked his identification card at me, and it landed on the ground outside of the car. Besides being rude, this was a dangerous officer safety issue. If I had bent down by his door to pick this up, I would have placed myself in an extremely vulnerable position and subjected myself to attack by this angry driver. I refused to pick it up. I backed away and asked the man to open his door and get out and retrieve it. He cursed at me, flung the door open and grabbed it. When he did, I noticed that he did not have any shoes on. He was completely barefoot.

When I asked him to hand his identification card to me again, he shoved it at me with his hand, and when I tried to grasp it, he wouldn't let go. He sarcastically declared, "I don't want you to drop it again." His insolence was really beginning to aggravate me. He was being a real jerk. Next, I asked for his insurance again. "I don't have insurance." He was batting a thousand with me, now.

Normally I would not write any driver more than two tickets. However, this was relatively early in my career, and I was not as professionally mature as I would become over the years. As a result, this guy's attitude sealed his fate that I would "stick it to him."

I sat in my car, seething because of this man's demeanor. Normally this type of foolishness did not bother me, but on this particular day, I was really not in the mood for sarcasm. I began writing. I wrote, and wrote, and wrote. I filled out three tickets for this man. I wrote him for expired inspection, no license, and no insurance. As I approached him to have him sign the citations and then release him, he began to curse at me. He was irate. He called me all sorts of names and insulted me and my family. At that point, he had gone too far. I completely lost my professionalism. I did not return his identification card to him. Instead, I told him to wait just another moment and I returned to my patrol vehicle where I began searching for another violation I could address with any additional citations.

I recalled having seen the man's bare feet as he exited the car to retrieve his identification. It was then that I let my better judgment escape me. I figured, "What the heck – he can take it to court!" I commenced to writing this driver a citation under the heading of "Other." The details of this citation would later flabbergast my sergeant as he reviewed the huge stack he had to process every night. I filled in the blank with the words "Driving without Shoes." After all, he was driving without shoes, and it looked really dangerous. He probably should not do that.

I returned to the vehicle and gave the man his extra ticket. He was so rude and angry that he didn't even look at the citation. As a matter of fact, he wadded it up and threw it into the floorboard of his car, along with the other three. I returned to my vehicle as he sped away. I was happy to see him go. What he chose to do with his citations was his problem.

They would turn into warrants if they remained in that floorboard. So be it.

The next night at roll call, my sergeant addressed our team as usual, but he had an extra item of business to discuss with us. He scooped the white copy of the citation I had written during the previous shift and held it up for all to see. He looked directly at me, and said, "What the heck is this? Driving without shoes – come on!"

Everyone in the room burst into laughter. That was obviously a ridiculous violation that did not even exist. No one knew yet who had written the ticket. It became clear, almost immediately, however, that it was me. Our sergeant then addressed me by my name, and asked, "What were you thinking? Where in the traffic law does it say a driver cannot drive without shoes? This is not even against the law!"

I knew he was right, but what could I do now? I certainly didn't expect to have the issue brought up in front of all of my peers, but I guess I deserved it. At the time, the violation sounded good. It came in especially handy when I was angry at this exceptionally rude driver. To this day, I still feel that even though driving barefoot is not against the Traffic Code, for that guy, it certainly should have been!

# Chapter Thirteen
## Working in Schools

One of my favorite periods of my career was when I worked for two years in the Youth Division as a Drug Abuse Resistance Education (D.A.R.E.) Officer. During this time I taught the drug education program to fifth graders full time. Teaching those kids was the best assignment I ever had within the police department. I loved the kids at that age. They were smart enough to understand what you were trying to tell them, but they had not yet reached that dreaded adolescent period where they hated authority and seemed to think they knew everything. We had a lot of fun together, and I enjoyed going to work every day. I would eat lunch with them, attend special field trips with them, and I even played football during recess with them. As a matter of fact, one time I was running so hard chasing an opponent that I fell and skinned up my knee. I felt just like one of the kids (until the next day when I couldn't get out of bed). I had a ball with them, and they thought I was cool. It was a very rewarding position.

Eventually our Department made the dreadful decision to abandon our D.A.R.E. program due to budget constraints. I had been in the unit for two years and had really enjoyed working with young people. As a result, when they offered me a position in the School Security Initiative Unit (S.S.I.), I was grateful to accept. The S.S.I. unit provided school resource officers to all middle and high schools within the Fort Worth Independent School District, and other schools that were in the Fort Worth City Limits. I would still be able to work in the schools, just with older students.

I spent the first full year of my new assignment as a "rover" which meant that I would substitute for officers in various schools who needed to be off work at different times. I found very quickly that many of the kids in middle school and high school *had* reached that dreaded adolescent period where they hated authority and seemed to think they knew everything. By the second year I was in this unit I had obviously lost my better judgment. For some mysterious reason I requested a position at an alternative ninth grade campus. This school is no longer in existence, but at the time, it was designed to help students who were behind in studies to catch up to the correct grade.

These students had a variety of personal issues going on in their lives, and none of them were simple. They spanned in age from fourteen to eighteen, and were all in the same grade. Consequently some of the younger students were exposed to some of the pre-maturely adult behaviors of the older students. Many of my students were in gangs; several used drugs, and most enjoyed a good fight on occasion. A lot of them had extensive juvenile criminal records, some were already parents, and all of them had academic challenges. This demographic was a difficult group for the school district to serve. It also proved to be quite a task for a police officer who was used to being loved by fifth grade D.A.R.E. students. In my new assignment, especially at this school, the police were not popular. As a matter of fact, I had become the enemy the moment I stepped through the door.

I love a challenge, so my mind began working towards solutions. I needed to figure out some way to create a solid rapport with these kids who had a preconceived negative notion about me. The mere presence of my uniform and badge was a barrier through which I would have to work diligently to break.

*I had the most challenging, yet rewarding times when I worked with the students who attended school in the City of Fort Worth. This was the photo I used for my D.A.R.E. trading cards that I used to give to my fifth grade students. (Photo by Alana Baxter)*

*There were definitely some benefits to working with fifth-graders! This was taken during a field trip with my Drug Abuse Resistance Education Students to the outdoor learning center. I was having a blast on the zip-line!*

# Good Report, Good Rapport

I have always been an encourager. I love to see the look on a person's face when he or she processes the feeling of receiving an uplifting comment. Knowing that encouragement is secretly desired by everyone, I looked for ways to uplift and edify the group of students who was struggling so fervently to make it from day to day in the alternative school where I had been assigned to work full-time. I prayed for the ability and the personal strength it would take to look beyond the overwhelming feelings of doom in the hallways during the passing periods. If I allowed myself to absorb the negative energy from that building, I would have been of no help to those kids. As a result, I whispered a personal prayer of courage and strength, and gulped down a breath of blessed assurance every time the bell rang. I stepped out into the hallway, ready to let my light shine into the lives of these at-risk students. Most were struggling through life during a time when they just happened to be victims of raging hormones, in addition to everything else they were trying to conquer.

The combination of these factors brewed negative behaviors and would inevitably spell trouble. Even so, there had to be some positive attributes in the building. There had to be some hope, and there had to be some dreams. It was my duty to find these hopes and dreams, extract them, and help cultivate them. It seemed as if almost no one else in these kids' lives would.

At the sound of the bell, teenagers would begin to fill the overcrowded, narrow hallways. As they passed by in groups, chattering, snickering and laughing, some would walk with friends, and others walked alone. There is a song about walking alone, and these kids personified the essence. In the eyes of those who were without companions, the most I could ever see was dread and emptiness. It made me sad.

Having made up my mind that I was going to find that elusive magical formula that would break through the wall of hatred this group had for law-enforcement, I created a plan. It was an experiment for this group, and I would attempt to conduct it without detection. As a result, I began an interesting course of observations that would give me the ability to explore the complex minds of my students.

I made it a point to listen to conversations as students passed in the hallway. I spent time in the cafeteria at breakfast and lunch-time and in the plaza with them during homeroom when they had free time. I vowed to learn the names of the kids one by one. I would spend a lot of time in the counselor's office listening and making mental notes as students registered. I spent an uncommon amount of time in the vice principal's office, because therein was another resource for learning names. He was in charge of the student identification cards. I would take the box of cards to the copy room as they were being processed. I would arrange ten student I.D. cards on a page and make a photocopy. I would study these pictures, and over time I was able to learn names of every single student in the building. I made sure that when disciplinary referrals were written, I knew about them. I began to develop a personal database of student names, behaviors, friends, clothing style, gang colors, and other important information *in my mind*. I did this for six years in a row, and it usually took me only two or three weeks to learn the nearly two-hundred students. Those first two weeks were a perfect opportunity for me to work on student identification and recognition while I began another equally important component to my plan. In order to begin the grueling task of building personal rapport during each and every passing period, as the students walked by, I would confidently and loudly say, "Good morning!" or "Good afternoon!" The most popular responses, at first, from the students were, "Drop dead," and "'F' off."

Just as I had suspected – this would be a hard group to reach. Even so, I was prepared. I have to admit that the negative reception was personally difficult for me, at first. I felt so stupid standing out there looking like "Suzy Sunshine" while these hard-core gangsters, drug dealers, and common criminals were walking by cursing and laughing at me. I had feelings, and they were a bit more damaged after every seven-minute passing period I endured. All things considered, I knew I had to be the mature adult. I was the one who was trying to exhibit godly wisdom and love for these kids. I was being ridiculed and persecuted for trying to have a good attitude in a building where bad attitude prevailed. That was okay. I would keep it up as long as it took. During the first couple of weeks, there was very little measurable change in the mindset of the students. I was the enemy, the bad guy, and it didn't look much like that was going to change. This was the same story, every year of the six that I spent at this school.

Each student had at least one or more personal reasons for being in this alternative school. That was strike number one. Many were unable to separate themselves from the personal behaviors that got them there in the first place, (gangs, drugs, alcohol, violence, theft, lack of motivation, broken families, and problems with authority – to name a few) and that was strike two. Finally, almost every student enrolled had a major deficit in learning abilities and struggled with school work. That was strike three. From the outside, it could easily have appeared that these kids were out of the running for a successful life. This school might have been perceived as having simply been a place to contain them while the school district "went through the motions" of educating them out of obligation.

Now I must say that the teachers and administrators did not feel this way, but there was some truth to the notion that some of these kids were not going to be the most successful people in our upcoming generation. Even after having been spoon fed study materials in non-challenging curriculums and having numerous opportunities to raise grades and to pass classes, some of these students just weren't cutting it. As a result, when the report cards came around, the building was overcome with even more of a melancholy-filled temperament.

This was my chance to take advantage of the negative mood in the building. I wondered what affect it would have if I could highlight the smallest victories of these students with some type of acknowledgement. I wanted to encourage each one, and develop relationships with as many as would allow me to. I used my creative motivation to develop a program for the students that would lend me the opportunity to interact with the kids. This would be fail proof. In a time when everyone around saw them as disappointments, I was going to point out the smallest of achievements and reward those efforts.

First, I moved an old bookshelf into my office. Next, I made a trip to some of my favorite local discount stores and shopped strategically for some items that would be of interest to the group of students in my school. I bought candy, mints, key chains, diaries, lip gloss, stuffed animals, chips, snacks, and even some school supplies like notebooks, pencils and folders. I spent wisely, and stocked my shelves full with these items, creating what looked like a little store in the corner of my office. Finally, I got permission to make an announcement during homeroom.

If a student passed all of his or her classes with a 70 or above, and had no unsatisfactory conduct marks, he or she could come to my office and choose a reward from the shelf. If a student made all "A's" and "B's," he or she could have two items. Lastly, if the student made straight "A's," he or she could have three items. This rarely happened, but when it did, the celebration rivaled that of winning a showcase showdown on "The Price is Right." They would get so excited to be allowed to choose two or three items.

My little reward store opened for business at the end of every six weeks. Essentially, if a student behaved acceptably and passed his or her classes, there would be a reward. You would be completely shocked at what a teenager will do for a Reese's Peanut Butter cup. I learned this from the movie, "Dangerous Minds." It works! The hard core gang members who were failing everything began to show up at my door after the second and third six weeks. They would proudly show me a report card where the grades had edged up from 65, 68, and 72 to 70, 75, and 78. They were trying, and they were improving. They were rewarded with their prize, and it made them proud.

Some of them vowed to be back next time with all "B's." They wanted to choose two items! I realized that it was not the thirty-cent candy bar that brought them into my office. Rather, it was the fact that they had someone who would give them positive affirmation for their efforts. They needed the encouragement, acknowledgment, acceptance and love.

I truly did begin to love these kids. The first contact with them had been in the hallway, being cursed and ridiculed. They had established reputations as criminals, trouble-makers, and slackers. Even so, I would always show respect as I would greet them. During those grading periods, I would lift up their accomplishments, proudly. Eventually, word got around that I was rewarding grades with cool stuff. I began to look forward anxiously to homeroom period on the day of report cards. Those were some of my favorite days at work during the school year. Over time, and with persistence, I had developed a genuine rapport and the ability to interact with these students in an amazingly effective manner. Eventually even the most hardened students began to respond to this program. Finally, I began to get through to the majority of the students. The relationships that began with cursing and hand-gestures were replaced with genuine smiles, words of greeting, and sometimes, even hugs. Most officers don't allow hugs from citizens or students, but in my case, I believed those hugs were a perfect opportunity to show love to these kids who hungered so for positive adult interaction. Eventually, a great number of the students were showing marked improvements in their grades. This was a victory for everyone.

After many long months of painstaking efforts to reach out, I was able to gain the trust of many of the students who were criminals. They would routinely come into my office and discuss their overwhelming temptations to use drugs, to steal, or to partake in gang activity. Peer pressure was a very real and difficult obstacle for them. Some of them already had children or had a baby on the way and they truly wanted to be a good parent. They wanted to graduate. They wanted to have a decent job someday. It quickly became clear to me that those elusive hopes and dreams were peeking out from the surface. They were trying so hard to emerge - to be reached and recognized. These aspirations began to surface privately as we would discuss various personal struggles in my office. Accountability developed as we discussed these issues and followed up with them weekly. I was now able to offer interventions instead of consequences. This was where I wanted to be. With God's help and guidance, I had prayerfully traveled the path that led me to success with these kids. I had struggled regularly, and it started all over again at the beginning of each new school year, but the rewards were ultimately priceless.

## The First Hurricane Katrina

One of the most challenging, yet rewarding students I have ever encountered is a female student who I will call "Katrina." She enrolled in the alternative school with anger management problems, irresponsible habits, family problems, emotional outbursts, and resentment for authority. She used profanity regularly without regard for anyone who might not want to hear it. One of the biggest problems in her life was the fact that she argued relentlessly with her mother on such a regular basis that I became well acquainted with her family and her home. I cannot count the times I had to go to this girl's house to intervene in domestic disputes between Katrina and her mom. I did not normally leave campus and deal with issues in the kids' personal homes or neighborhoods, but this girl quickly became special to me. She needed some focused attention, and I could tell that despite all of her faults, she had a loving heart and a desire to change for the better. She was misdirected, hurt, and involved in a constant struggle to make it from day to day. She had poor decision-making skills and would often become very frustrated after making a bad choice. The first couple of times I spoke with her, I was bombarded with a string of profanity. By this time I had been working in the alternative school culture for several years. I had developed an appreciation for the fact that until I had a chance to acquaint myself with each student, my presence would usually be met with resistance, often in the form of cursing and gnashing of teeth.

Katrina was an angry girl. Her heart was as turbulent as a category five hurricane. She had personal turmoil inside her that would have to be peeled away in bitter, stinging layers, much like those of an onion. Her pain ran deep, and her ability to cope was practically non-existent. Her misery quickly became my calling. I developed a genuine love for Katrina, and when she would have a temper flare-up, I was the only one to whom she would respond. I would be very firm with her, but she usually did what I asked her to do.

Our relationship blossomed because one of the first times I ever saw her, even after having been cursed by her, I explained to her that I was a Christian. I told her that I would not judge her for her behavior, and that I would always be fair in my actions with her. I told her that I would pray for her, because I could see that she had a lot of anger and pain. I did not allow her to use these things as an excuse, but I did acknowledge her issues. She appreciated this, and as a result, a very solid bond was cultivated between us. Our relationship truly blossomed, and I was thankful.

After several trips to her home to pick her up and bring her to school in the mornings (after arguments with her mother), and after several interventions in the office to keep her from being suspended, Katrina and I had developed a very strong relationship. She began working hard to improve her grades. Her outbursts were less frequent, and when she had them, she was calmed more easily. One day while we were talking in my office, the subject of "right and wrong" emerged. She and I discussed the fact that although people usually know the difference between right and wrong, our sinful nature often allows us to make the wrong choice.

Katrina desperately wanted help. She desired to make better choices. She wanted to conquer the desire to choose wrong. I told her who could help her. I pulled my personal bible out of my briefcase and began showing Katrina the verses that illustrate the fall of mankind. I then showed her that Jesus was born and grew up as a perfect and sinless man. I explained how He took the burden of sin from us through His crucifixion. We then travelled through the book of Romans and talked about salvation, methodically reading the verses that explain God's love, His provision, and His forgiveness. That day in my office, Katrina and I bowed our heads in prayer. I guided her as she asked forgiveness for her sins, and received the precious gift of salvation from our Lord, Jesus Christ. She raised her head from her prayer and exclaimed to me, "I am changed. I am saved. I can do this, now!" Those words, accompanied by the amazing sparkle in her eyes, were probably the most precious ones ever uttered to me during my entire fifteen-year career. I was given the privilege and the opportunity to lead my precious girl Katrina to the Lord, and she truly desired a relationship with Him.

The very next day, I brought Katrina her own study bible for teenagers. She was elated to have God's Word in her possession. She had a hunger to learn about God, and about His amazing love for us, as humans. I was impressed to see that over the next several months, Katrina carried that bible in her backpack with her, every day. Often, she would bring it to my office and open it. The pages were covered with yellow highlights. She was reading it! She was learning it. She was trying to live it. Katrina would select a passage and ask me to help her understand it. I was so overwhelmed by her newfound hunger for Christ that my joy was uncontainable. All of the negative energy had left the building, at least from my perspective!

I must qualify this account by admitting that Katrina did not transform overnight into a perfect angel. However, her desires to change did have quite a positive influence on her behavior, which markedly increased her success. I have tried to maintain contact with Katrina throughout the years, but we have lost touch. The last time I saw her she had just graduated from a charter high school, and had a newborn baby boy. I wish I could find her today to see how she is doing. Even though that is probably impossible for now, at least I know with certainty that we will meet again. Thanks to our time together with God's word, and her decision to accept the gift of salvation, I know that one day I will see her again, in Heaven, and for now, that's good enough for me.

# Hide and Seek
*[This story discusses drug, alcohol and sexual paraphernalia]*

I could easily understand why students did not want to associate with me. It became clear that the activities they enjoyed were not congruent with hanging around with a police officer. Over the course of my six years in that same alternative school, I found countless pieces of evidence that confirmed my suspicions about the clandestine behaviors the students enjoyed. These teenagers obviously could not make it through the day separated from the contraband they needed in order to carry out their mischief. Instead, they had to bring it to school and try to find a way to hide it for the day. Despite our intermittent attempts at random searches and our sporadic use of metal detectors, a truckload of contraband per day undoubtedly made it into that building. I was not ignorant to that reality. As a matter of fact, it was something I was quite well aware of, and that truth provided me with daily entertainment. At first I felt personally defeated as I would locate these items on a very regular basis. Then it became clear to me that with a student population of almost 200 at-risk students and a clearly insufficient number of staff members, there was no way to come out victorious in the daily battle of the contraband. However, I could certainly have fun trying.

I would routinely patrol the campus, both indoors and out, while class was in session, looking for the hidden illegal items. Those kids had some creative hiding places. They would dig holes and bury things, hide items behind shrubs, cover them with leaves, place them in drain pipes, stuff them in cracks in the bricks, hide them behind doors to fuse boxes, climb the gazebo behind the school and put them up on the rafters, and they would even remove covers from ventilation ducts if they could get the screws loose. These creative methods of concealment paled in comparison, however, to the removal of ceiling tiles in the restrooms. This dark attic space was the perfect place for them to hide smuggled goods. Desperate students would climb up onto the toilet seat inside a stall and lift a Styrofoam ceiling tile. This would open up a seemingly perfect place to stash just about anything one could imagine. I have always been fascinated with the dynamics of criminal thinking. Unfortunately, young criminal minds seem to have a creative flair that represents a vast waste of what could otherwise be remarkable talent.

The list of smuggled goods I found hidden over the course of my assignment at this particular school is extensive. When I narrow it down to items found in the ceiling tiles alone, it is staggering:

- A 40 ounce bottle of beer
- A bottle of whiskey
- A stack of pornographic magazines
- Cigarettes and lighters
- Permanent markers that had been used to graffiti the school
- Stink bombs
- Pocket knives
- Stolen test answer-keys
- A wallet and credit cards stolen from a teacher's locked cabinet
- A stolen cell phone
- Marijuana
- Rolling papers
- Condoms

All of these items were found during random sweeps of the campus, because the workload did not allow me the opportunity to do this every day. I would routinely ask the vice principal, campus monitor or the custodian to accompany me into the restrooms during class time. We would lock the doors behind us and begin the treasure hunt. It was always fun, except for the fact that I would have to stand on the toilet and try not to fall as I lifted the Styrofoam ceiling tile. As I would feel around the area just around the edge of the opening, more often than not there would be something illegal, dangerous, or both, hidden in the ceiling.

To top off the fun, I would enjoy standing near the restrooms after the bell so I could watch the students go in after school to attempt to retrieve items they had stashed for the day. When their stuff was gone, it was almost impossible for them to hide the anger and aggravation as they exited the restroom. They never knew it was me who removed their stuff. As a matter of fact, they would sometimes spend the next few days accusing friends and acquaintances of taking it.

# Mustard Marinated Cigarettes
*[This story discusses drug use and paraphernalia]*

Working as a school resource officer at another one of my several assigned alternative schools during my tour with the School Security Initiative Unit, I found a unique, yet extremely entertaining way to spread a subliminal message to students about the ills of hiding contraband. At this particular school, several different educational programs were housed on one campus. Some students were delivered from all over town via public transportation, while others used the school district buses. The area where students were dropped off by the city bus was about two blocks from the actual school location. As a result, that two-block trek to the campus was their last bounty of freedom before they entered a day of following rules and taking orders. Because of their perception of the impending doom that awaited them at the educational establishment around the corner, this journey often became one that would lend itself to temptation.

The number of students would customarily drop by four or five from the time the group exited the bus to the time they walked onto the property of the school complex. The ones who fell from the ranks, succumbing to the pressure, had stopped behind one of the local businesses to smoke one last cigarette or marijuana joint. Either that or they simply had to take one last swig of the liquor or other alcoholic beverage that had been smuggled underneath their loosely fitting jacket. Finally, and most importantly, they had to find the perfect niche along the landscape scenery along the way where they could safely and strategically place their pocket knives, lighters, condoms, and prescription bottles containing their other elicit drugs and contraband.

As part of my job on most mornings I would leave my marked patrol vehicle parked prominently in the parking lot in front of the school, close to where the district buses would drop kids off. The presence of my vehicle there prompted students to believe that I was somewhere nearby, thus deterring a great deal of shenanigans. While my car served as quasi-proof of my presence there, I would take the winding path behind the cafeteria, between shrubs, trees and concrete retaining walls and walk to a nearby fast food restaurant that overlooked the path of the city bus students' trek to the school. You're probably thinking that it was pretty irresponsible of my to leave the school during a crucial time to go have breakfast. Well, bear with me. Actually, breakfast was the furthest thing from my mind. This was because I had a more sinister, plan that would be much more satisfying than biscuits, gravy, and coffee.

Believe it or not, I was actually there to conduct surveillance and gather information. I would normally sit by a window, obscured by the advertisements hanging or written on the panes. From this perch, I was able to see things that would provide me with much needed strategic intelligence that would make my life much, much easier later during the day while inside the school.

For example, I could watch as a certain individual would hide a lighter and a package of rolling papers behind a shrub by a brick wall on the path. I could see another reach up and place a pocket knife in the crook of a tree. I secretly observed a third disappear behind the fence that masked the dumpster behind the eating establishment. A couple of seconds later, that student joined the rest of the group that had decided to actually go to school for the day. I would sit in different places every morning, finding new perspectives to spy on my students. I did not feel the least bit guilty sneaking around. After all, they knew that whatever they were hiding was off limits, illegal or against school policy. It was my job to keep the school safe, so my awareness of who was involved in what types of extracurricular habits was just one aspect of my duty to provide good security for the campus.

Watching and taking note of who ditched what and where was pretty helpful for getting a perspective on the thought processes of the kids. This was especially true when I was asked to perform an evaluation on a student to determine if he or she was under the influence of a drug or alcohol. Having seen them ditch their rolling papers, pipes and lighters before school gave me some added confidence that this student was indeed impaired. Even so, I never let them know that I was aware of these outside factors.

This type of logic was also helpful when a student would become involved in violent behavior during the day. It was good to know that he or she expected to have access to a pocket knife that they believed was hidden in a tree behind the school. If they were involved in a physical confrontation on campus, they may have planned to retrieve that hidden weapon after school and do more violence. The fact that I had possession of the weapon, even though they didn't yet know it, was comforting. Believe me, nothing was beyond the scope of what some of these kids would do. Many of them were being monitored by juvenile probation, and many more of them *should have been.*

It was not uncommon for students to meet up before school and walk in large groups to locations near the school to engage in gang fights. These kids, coming from all over town, would undoubtedly clash with someone from another community while confined to the one alternative campus which was centrally located. During the times when we suspected such activity, I would patrol the area, taking the senior campus monitor with me. We would drive around and keep an eye on the factions that would gather, prodding them towards the school by circling the block, relentlessly. When one group would finally be ushered onto the campus, it was time to guide another. These kids were like marbles, they would roll all over the place if we didn't funnel them to the right destination.

On the days when I needed to stay in the car, I found places to hide in it, too. It was especially fun when the campus monitor was with me, because he knew stories about each student, and would give me a profile as each would pass by. We would sit and laugh as kid after kid would exit the bus, run to the brick retaining wall bordered by shrubbery, and hide their prohibited items in that perfect, special spot. Little did they know they were being stalked by forces more ruthless than even they could imagine.

Considering all of the trouble these delinquents would bring to us on a daily basis, we enjoyed the concept of getting even in a way that would perplex the students, and that would keep us obscured from any suspicion, whatsoever. Remember, we had a virtual treasure map of hidden contraband by the time school was actually in session. This was when the second stage of the fun would start. My campus monitor was an older gentleman who had worked with kids for decades. He had an uncanny ability to connect with even the most hardened adolescent minds. Despite his tough demeanor, he was well liked because he dealt with students respectfully and with genuine concern. Even so, this man had a mean streak in him that most definitely needed to be kept under wraps as a secret weapon. As a means of release for his brilliance, we decided to have a little fun with one of those who chose to ditch prohibited items along the path to school.

My usual routine was to walk the trail of hidden items and sporadically remove certain items from their cover. I did not take everything I knew about because I did not want the kids to recognize a developing pattern of their items being taken every day. I just took random items and discarded them into the dumpster. After all, technically, these items were abandoned. There is no expectation of security when someone stashes items behind a shrub on a public sidewalk, or in a tree behind a strip mall. Anyone in the community could have seen it being placed there. I always kept those students guessing, and I enjoyed it, immensely. Sometimes I would take the cigarettes and lighters, other times I would leave them. I would always take the drugs and rolling papers and destroy them. If I saw a student hide a weapon such as a pocket knife, I would always take it. A pocket knife is not illegal, but I would never leave anything behind that could have inflicted injury upon another person. After all, it was during the bus rides home that a great deal of our violence would occur between rival students. There is no way I would allow a student to retrieve a weapon and enter the bus after school. However, there were things that I would do; things that would not jeopardize the safety of anyone – yet still things that I probably shouldn't have done.

One morning my brilliant campus monitor was accompanying me on a routine patrol of the area surrounding the school. We watched the daily ritual as the students hid their stuff and continued, without a care, on their trek to school. We had been inside the fast food restaurant, and he had acquired some of those little packets of ketchup and mustard. Having watched a particularly difficult and incorrigible student hide his stash by the dumpster behind the restaurant, we decided that he was our perfect candidate for a surprise at the end of the school day.

When we were sure all students were gone from the area, I approached the hiding place and retrieved his almost full pack of cigarettes from behind the dumpster. It included a lighter stuffed down inside the packaging. I returned to the car where we executed our evil plan. I emptied the lighter and the cigarettes from the package. He opened three or four packets of mustard. When the box was empty, he squirted the packets into the box, filling it about one-fourth the way full of sour, yellow, runny mustard. We hoped the condiment would enhance the pleasurable effects of the cigarettes for our student when he returned at the end of the day. I placed the cigarettes back neatly into the pack, one by one, along with the lighter, which I inserted face-down into the box. After we marinated the cigarettes and the lighter for this student, I returned them carefully to the spot from which I had found them. I then laughed with my partner in crime as we returned to the school to deal with the entire group of indignant students who would try to make our day miserable.

No matter what those kids did to try to aggravate us that day, nothing could break our spirit. We had a secret, and although it was childish, it was magnificent. The only drawback was the fact that I would probably not be available at the end of the day to see the reaction when this student found his spicy, yellow cigarettes. Unfortunately for me, I was usually busy from the time I entered the campus every day until the time I left. Thankfully, however, my vivid imagination was sufficient for me to develop a mental picture of what this kid's face might look like when he returned for his smokes.

Although I did not get to see him, I did routinely get to watch some of the others as they would head back towards the city bus on the way home. As they would stop to pick up their contraband it was genuinely funny to see the perplexed looks as they would search the area. It was clear they wondered if they were searching in the right place for their rolling papers, lighters, condoms, and whatever else they had ditched earlier in the day. It was an extremely entertaining way for me to alleviate some of the stress of dealing with the delinquents whose sole purpose was to make my life miserable. I realized it was immature and could be considered somewhat unprofessional, but it sure was fun!

## Keys in the Car

Perhaps nothing can be more inconvenient and embarrassing than locking the keys in your car. The effect is exponential when you are a police officer, in full uniform, working at an alternative high school, and *your car is running*. Add to this a temperature of about 35 degrees (in Texas, this is really cold) and me having to stand outside guarding my car in order to avoid its being stolen by one of my students!

This actually happened to me once (and after once I can assure you it would never, ever happen again) as I was arriving to work as the school resource officer at a ninth grade alternative school campus. It is impossible to leave the vehicle unattended when the keys are pristinely displayed in the ignition, and when exhaust fumes are flowing freely. I had a certain reserved parking spot that was in the path where students walked as they were dropped off for school. It was obviously very cold, and my standing outside the driver's side door looked a bit suspicious, especially in the mind of a teenager who would love to go for a joyride in a patrol car instead of attending alternative school.

As a result of my ignorance, I had to get on the police radio (my cell phone was in my briefcase, locked inside the car) and attempt to locate one of my fellow officers who was close. When I located someone close, I had to pray that they would be able to drop everything and come to help me. Next, I had to get them to go to a side channel on the radio where hopefully not too many other officers would follow to listen. Then, I had to confess to this officer that I was an idiot, and that I had locked my keys in my running car. Finally, I had to beg them to hurry because I was freezing. This was not a series of tasks I was eager to endeavor. However, I was pretty desperate, and short of paying to replace a broken window, that was my only option.

As I stood out there on the radio trying to contact someone who might have a key to my car, I looked up towards the second floor of the school. Through a window to a classroom I saw an increasing number of students gathering to point and laugh at me. They waved. I waved back. I acted like it was no big deal, but I was really terribly embarrassed. I was not supposed to do stupid stuff like this. Besides all that, it was almost freezing out there.

Then the thought hit me. If those kids decided to get into a fight (which occurred rather often) I would be standing out by my car, unable to leave, waiting for a key. These kids were prone to starting riots, smoking pot in the restrooms, burglarizing snack vending machines and other creative behaviors, especially first thing in the morning. I could imagine me trying to explain to my supervisor how all this could happen - kids wreaking havoc inside my school building while I stood outside by my patrol vehicle. Luckily and thankfully the kids who knew of my predicament at the time were not the ones who were inclined to take advantage of my compromising position.

I called my friend who happened to live close by. She did not have to report for work until a bit later. As a result, she was still at home.

Thankfully, she was getting ready to walk out the door, anyway, so she was able to come very quickly. Even so, the feeling of discomfort was building with every minute I had to wait for her. I waited about fifteen minutes, but it seemed like an eternity, as I had to continually field questions from the students who were arriving for school, walking past me. Despite my complete humiliation, my friend came through for me and I suffered only minimal ridicule from these fifteen year olds when I finally made it inside the school.

## Burning House!
*[This story mentions drug use]*

Working at the alternative high school, it became necessary to spend quite a bit of time outside of the school monitoring the neighborhood. It was not uncommon for my crafty students to sneak out the back door and try to blend into the community. They would walk around and seek places to hide and spend the hours smoking, drinking, and simply avoiding school, in general. Often they would graffiti fences and steal various items that weren't tied down. As a result, I became acquainted with some of the residents who lived in the homes around the school. One man who lived nearby even had my cell phone number. When some of my students would skip and hide in the alley behind his house, he would call me and tell me about it. The kids never knew that I had operatives in the community watching out for suspicious activity. They always seemed surprised when I would show up with a couple of other officers ready to arrest them while they were right in the middle of smoking their marijuana. I routinely caught them in the alleys, in abandoned houses, and even in a broken down garage within a block of the school. My success in this regard was due, in part, to those tips from the citizens.

One day I was heading from the school building to my car for my routine patrol outside the school. I noticed that there was a thick plume of dark colored smoke coming from a home in the block right behind the school. I knew the family who lived in this home as one who regularly walked up and down the block to access the nearby convenience store. I would often see the man, woman, and their small boy walking in the neighborhood. The little boy was adorable, and he always waved at me when I would see him.

The home was a duplex, and the family I knew lived on the right side of the property. Unfortunately, this was the side from which the very dark mass of smoke was emanating. The smoke was so thick that it immediately captured my attention. The duplex did not have a fireplace, but the smoke was coming right from the center of the top of the house. It actually appeared to be originating from the attic. An adrenaline rush of near panic swept over me, because I knew that the family was typically home during the day. I called the Fort Worth Fire Department immediately to get them started on the way. Then, I got in my patrol car and drove to the front of the house, just a few yards behind the school on the opposite side of the road.

From this vantage point, I could tell that the smoke was violently billowing from the attic, and it was getting worse by the second. I exited the car and ran to the front porch. Here I was able to access the front doors of both duplex apartments. I banged on the doors as hard as I could. There was a man whom I did not know who came to the front door on the left side of the duplex-home. I told him the house was on fire, and he needed to get out. He was dumbfounded, and stalled for a bit. I told him to hurry, that there was a family on the other side of the building that needed to be warned. This man ran back inside to grab some jeans and his wallet. He then started trying to gather other items on the way out. I became stern with him and walked inside a few feet and grabbed him by the arm. I told him that he had to get out, immediately. When I pulled him out of the front door, he could then see how bad things were and he ran away from the structure to safety.

On the right side of the duplex I continually banged on the door and still did not get a response. I even kicked it a few times, trying to break it down. This neighborhood, unfortunately, was one where the citizens felt the need to fortify their homes for their personal safety. As a result, this door was bolted so well that I would need a battering ram to open it.

The smoke became thicker, and I could tell that it wouldn't be long before the home began to collapse as it became more and more engulfed in flames. I still could not locate the people inside, and I had an incredibly strong feeling that they were home. The only thing left to do was to travel the circumference of the home banging on the windows, trying to stir someone inside. Finally, when I got to the rear of the home, there was a back door and a window. The curtain was positioned perfectly against the window in a manner that allowed me to see inside. It was then I discovered that the people were asleep on their bed in this back room. I was mortified. The smoke was closer to the front of the home, but I knew that they were in grave danger, even if they weren't already affected by smoke inhalation. I banged on the door and actually tried to kick it open. The door was apparently barred closed because it was not normally used. It even had a parcel of furniture blocking it. However, the family began to stir, and I was able to yell through the window that they were in danger.

The man stumbled to the window half-asleep and opened it. I told him that his home was on fire, and that he needed to get out immediately. He could see the smoke billowing more from the outside than from the inside, because it was coming from directly above us, now. He could tell that it was an urgent situation. He ran back into the home and grabbed his little boy, the one who I had waved to so many times before. The child was startled by all of the commotion that woke him from his sound sleep. He was wrapped in a blanket and screaming with fear as the man handed him to me through the opened window. He begged me to take his boy to safety. I told him I would, but I directed him and his wife to get out of the house, immediately, as well. He assured me that they would climb out of the window, but both he and his wife wanted to grab some personal items from the home. I urgently exclaimed to him that salvaging personal property was not going to be possible. The woman desperately wanted to find her purse, which I understood completely. However, this fire had been burning for awhile, and the ceiling could have collapsed at any time. I ordered them to get out of the home, and watched as they began to crawl out, reluctantly, with nothing more than what they were wearing and a couple of blankets. I could empathize with them wanting to gather some personal items, but there was not enough time. I felt horribly for them, having been awakened by such a tragic incident. I cannot imagine being startled from a sound sleep with absolutely no time to gather anything from my home. What a horrible experience that must have been. Adding to it was the fact that they were in extremely dire risk of imminent death. When I was sure the couple was actually moving towards exiting the house through the window, I carried the little boy out to my car in the front of the house and put him safely inside. The smoke was getting pretty thick, and even the air outside was getting hard to breathe. The fire trucks were just arriving, and while they were pulling up, the man and his wife were finally getting out of the window in the back.

The flames began to lap outside of the roof of the house from the attic area. Even though this poor family did not have time to get any of their belongings out of the home, I was thankful that they were alive. I knew that God's perfect provision had allowed me to be in the right place at the right time to see that smoke when the mysterious fire first began. Had I not been in the place to see it right when I did, the family may not have survived. They were sound asleep in the back of the house, and had no idea it was burning. I remember distinctly my heartfelt "thank you" prayer to God. I was so grateful to Him for allowing everyone to escape without harm. Later I began thinking about the reason I was outside the school in the first place. It was because of my delinquent students. Ironically, the routine criminal antics of those kids had a part in saving this family. If I had not been accustomed to searching for kids who normally snuck out the back of the school to skip and terrorize the neighborhood, I would probably not have been out there that day. This just proves to me that if we ponder them long enough, even the worst of situations can somehow be looked upon as a form of God's perfect wisdom and providence.

## A "Heartfelt" Friendship
*[This story depicts slightly graphic violence]*

When I think about it, this story still makes me cringe. At the alternative school we used to set up random metal detector details in the hallway during the school day. We would run the students through it for safety purposes a couple of times a month. The students never knew when we were going to have one, so it was theoretically supposed to be a deterrent against weapons and contraband. We usually ended up with a shoe-box full of confiscated banned items like lighters, markers, and cigarettes during these sweeps, but not much more.

One day when we conducted a routine metal detector detail the students were lining up to leave the classroom. During this time, one student who I will call "Wallace" removed a pocket knife from his jacket. He knew it was against school policy and he would be expelled if caught with it. As a result, he hid it behind a computer monitor in the classroom.

Keep in mind, we knew kids always dumped things as they

were lining up, so we instructed the teachers stay in the classroom and play "hide and seek" while the kids were gone. They would find all sorts of goodies while the students were out in the hallway waiting to walk through. The students expected to come back into the room and reclaim their contraband. I had several teachers who would provide me with abandoned drugs, knives, lighters, and markers that they found stashed in the room while the students were participating in the detail outside in the hall.

On this day, however, when Wallace ditched his knife, a fellow student who I will call "Earnest" grabbed it from its hiding place, and apparently hid it in a better place where the teacher could not find it. After the class had gone through the detector the students all returned to the room. Wallace began looking for his pocket knife, and realized it had been moved. Then Earnest pulled it from its new hiding place, and showed it to the Wallace, mocking him by refusing to return it. Although these kids were friends, the fact that his knife was being held hostage made Wallace a bit upset. This fueled Earnest even more, so he opened the knife up and started taunting Wallace again by holding it up and pulling it out of reach of Wallace's hands as he attempted to grab it. This aggravated Wallace further still, so he jumped towards Earnest and the two began scuffling over the knife. [In case you are wondering, the teacher was in the room at the time. However, she thought the two were just play-fighting because they usually got along well.]

The teacher finally directed the two to stop playing around. It was only then that she realized that they were both actually agitated, and they were really fighting. As a result, she wrote them up on disciplinary referral forms and sent them both to the vice principal. I usually worked with the administrators on these types of incidents. Normally I would issue citations for classroom disruptions or disorderly conduct-fighting when merited. However, in this instance the vice principal decided not to pursue the citations for these students because neither one of them usually caused any trouble. He decided to simply call parents and send them both home for the rest of the day to cool off.

Wallace's mom worked nearby and was there to pick him up within about ten minutes. Earnest, on the other hand, had to stick around a bit waiting for his ride. Even so, I considered this situation to be diffused because the two students had been separated and one of them was no longer on campus. Nevertheless, I did not even get halfway back to my office before the principal summonsed me, via the school radio. Upon my arrival at his office, I learned that Wallace was in the emergency room at Harris Hospital. He had been stabbed in the chest, and the knife had nicked his heart.

We were all in shock, because we did not know how he had been stabbed, or even *that* he had been stabbed. He never said a word to anyone about being hurt while he was still at the school. During the scuffle we had no idea that there had been a knife involved. The only ones who knew about the knife were Wallace and Earnest. Because Earnest was still on campus, he was questioned about what happened. The vice principal told him that Wallace had been stabbed in the heart. Earnest turned pale white and looked ill. He immediately admitted that he and Wallace had been scuffling over a knife that he had in his pocket. He produced the knife, which was closed. It did not have any blood on the blade, but it was about two and a half inches long. Earnest described how he had the knife opened during the scuffle. He remembered poking at Wallace with it and making contact with his clothing. However, he did not know it had punctured Wallace's skin.

Actually, even Wallace was reluctant to tell what had happened because he did not want Earnest to get into trouble. Furthermore, he did not want to get into trouble, either. After all, the knife involved was *his knife* to begin with. Consequently, he decided not to say anything about what he thought was a small nick to the skin on his chest. That was until he was in the car with his mom and noticed a large amount of blood beginning to soak through his shirt and jacket. The sight of the blood frightened him and made him queasy. It was only then that he told his mom he thought he had been stabbed. She was mortified, and when she asked what happened, he said another student stuck him during the fight at the school. Wallace's mom immediately took him to the emergency room, where he was now being evaluated.

The principal asked me to accompany him to check on Wallace, and when we got there, we learned that he would have to undergo a minor surgery to stitch up the outer lining of the heart which had been nicked by the knife. After some stitches and a tetanus shot, thankfully Wallace would be heading home later that night. We were able to speak with him briefly, and he adamantly refused to press aggravated assault charges on

Earnest. Even so, Earnest would have to face expulsion for the incident, and believe it or not, so would Wallace. This is a perfect example of why pocket knives must now be banned from the school setting.

## Our Future Engineers
*[This story depicts drug use and paraphernalia]*

The phenomenon of wasted talent became all the more apparent to me when I surveyed some of the homemade bongs the students hid around the campus. They obviously had to smoke their marijuana on such a regular basis, both in and out of school, that they had to have a spare bong at their disposal. I found several creative examples during my watch there. One of the simplest was crafted from an empty bottle of hair-color, a straw and some foil. Another was made from a plastic soda bottle, chewed gum, and a straw. I found more than a few soda cans that had holes punched in them, complete with burned residue. Some students didn't need anything more than a sheet of foil. They molded and shaped foil into very interesting contraptions, all for the purpose of smoking dope. Others really liked the duct-tape theory. Duct tape will work on anything – even a double bong made from a soda can and two straws. I wouldn't believe some of these gadgets were operational, but each of them held signs of the telltale residue and odor of burned marijuana. I could never help thinking to myself, "If these students would spend only a *fraction* of the time and effort they put into creating a bong out of a soda bottle, and instead focused on a legitimate goal, they would be geniuses!"

Unfortunately, it was impossible for me and the administrators to be everywhere we needed to be at one time. The task of catching all of the students who smoked between classes was impossible. When the bell would ring, several students would run out the back door and hunch behind cars, hide in the bushes, and even scamper into the fire-exit emergency stair wells. Of course the tell-tale smoke would waft out into the common areas of the school eventually, but by that time the students were back in the classroom, doused with cologne to cover the tell-tale odor. Before we knew it, several students suddenly became entertained, amused and awestruck by sentence structure and math equations as their teachers began class.

## Mercury Mayhem

My assignment to this alternative school was such a challenging episode that I could absolutely write volumes on my daily adventures there. Believe it or not, the incident I am about to describe actually represents the types of occurrences that happened during a somewhat normal day at this school. Even so, I cannot overlook the sheer mass of ignorance which was rampant in the midst of this population of student delinquents. On this particular day I was summonsed to the vice principal's office because he needed to inform me of a critical incident. He proceeded to inform me that some of our students had been playing with mercury in a classroom. That's right, mercury. A student brought a vial of it to school. Its origin was a mystery, but he was having a stellar time dropping it on the floor, watching it break into little silver bb-sized clumps that rolled under the desks and all over the classroom floor. I was absolutely dumbfounded to learn that we actually had a group of kids playing with mercury in the school. It was hard for anything to surprise me at this campus, but honestly, the mercury – that got me. Because we did not have an extensive science lab full of chemicals, I never expected to have a hazardous material incident, even at this crazy school! Apparently this student had poured it out onto his desk to impress several of the other students. When it broke up into pieces and rolled around, they were all having a ball trying to collect it and build it into one big clump again. They were playing with it in their bare hands.

We ended up calling the fire department to conduct a hazardous material cleanup and investigation. Luckily this was their specialty. The students who handled the mercury had to disrobe and go through a decontamination process. They had to wear white paper suits and call parents to come to the school. The fire department gave them further instructions on how to recognize possible symptoms of mercury poisoning. They confiscated the mercury, and practically tore up the classroom trying to make sure they got it all. We had to hold the bells from the passing periods for hours because we could not allow any other students to be introduced to the area where they might be exposed. It was truly a nightmare. The uninvolved students thought it was cool to miss their classes, but the students who had been exposed were actually mortified. They had no idea that they were handling a very dangerous chemical. God only knows where it came from, and I am glad of that fact. I don't think I want to know the answer to that one. This was just another fine example of life in an alternative school.

## Teeny Who-Deeny

I was working at a different alternative high school when I received a call to the office regarding a student who was belligerent and out of control. Upon my arrival, I could hear this young man cursing and yelling as he sat in a conference room with a campus monitor. I learned that he had been disruptive in his class, causing enough of a ruckus to receive a disciplinary referral. As a result, the administrators requested that I issue a citation to this young man. In a domino-effect sequence of events, the citation revoked his probation. This school staff customarily used what would normally be considered minor infractions as an excuse to remove students from the population, especially when the student routinely displayed negative behavior.

When I saw this young man, I couldn't help but notice how small-framed he was. He was probably about 5'5" and weighed around 140 lbs. I remained cautious because I had learned that with adolescents, strength or ability to fight cannot be determined by the size of the kid. Besides that, this student had a reputation for being extremely violent, and the administrators wanted me to arrest him on his probation violation and then transport him to the juvenile detention center.

I knew from the very beginning that this was not going to be easy. This kid was angry, wiry, and strong. He was already agitated, had been on probation, and he vigorously hated the police. Now he would be sent back to detention for several days as a result of this seemingly minor violation. I called for an assist unit because I suspected I may have trouble with this arrest. I would need someone nearby to back me up while I took this young man into custody.

When it was time to effect the arrest, I realized that my gut instinct had been correct. It took quite a fight, complete with cursing, spitting, punching, kicking, struggling and the work of two officers to get him handcuffed. When he began kicking at us, we naturally assumed that he would also be kicking at the windows of the patrol car. We made the decision to place leg restraints on him so he would not break out the window and harm himself with the broken glass. He was jerking away from both of us as we were walking him to patrol the vehicle. When we got to the parking lot, a staff member from the school brought us a pair of leg restraints, as I had requested. When the student saw these, he became even more enraged.

As helpful as leg restraints can be, there is an obvious problem with getting them on a subject. This would be a challenge today, as well, because this kid would not stop kicking and fighting. While the other officer secured the student from his upper body area, I had to lean down to the ground and try to get the leg restraints on him, dodging blows to my upper torso, face, and head. It took two staff members from the school, the other officer, and me to hold the kid still. This was before I had even attempted to put the cuffs around his legs.

The next thing we all realized was that while we were working so diligently on restraining his legs, he had squeezed out of one of his handcuffs. He began to fling the cuff at all of us around him. Immediately we regained control of him and were able to handcuff him again. After that, we put a second pair of handcuffs on him, while still working to get the leg restraints secured. This kid was probably fifteen years old, and was violent, strong and angry enough that four adults were struggling to keep him under control.

Eventually, I was able to get one of the leg restraints on, and finally the second one. He still kicked, but was not able to kick more than a foot or so with the chain tethering his two legs together at the ankles. Next was the task of getting him into the vehicle. The F.W.P.D. has a very strict policy against hog-tying a suspect, which is restraining the arms and legs, and then connecting them together with another pair of handcuffs behind the suspect's back. This would not be possible under any circumstances, most especially not with a youth.

In order to solve the problem of getting him into the vehicle, a third officer who had arrived on the scene got on the passenger side of the back seat of the car while the other four of us picked up this wiry little angry kid. Keep in mind he was double-handcuffed and wearing leg restraints. We directed him into the back of the car like a spear. We sent him headfirst through the door and into the passenger compartment. He was then intercepted by the third officer who helped to sit him up in the car. Luckily the vehicle we were using had an eyebolt in the floor designed to attach the leg restraints to the floor. This was to prevent arrested persons from leaning up and kicking the windows out with both legs. We connected the metal clip that secured the young man's leg restraints down in the floorboard area. Finally, we maneuvered the seatbelt around him and were set to go. He was double handcuffed, leg restraints were applied and those were then bolted to the floor, and he was seat-belted into the back seat of a patrol car with a full plastic cage shielding the front half from the back half of the passenger compartment.

The student was in my assist officer's car, and my partner was going to drive to the detention center while I followed. We began our journey and exited the parking lot. The third assist officer left the scene in anticipation of returning to her school. We got two blocks down the road and to the service road of the freeway when I noticed the young man wriggling around in the back seat of my partner's car up ahead of me. The next thing I knew, I heard his voice on the police radio advising me that he was going to have to pull over. This kid had squeezed out from both pairs of handcuffs, loosened his seatbelt *and* the connection to the eyebolt. The only thing keeping him from being completely free was the leg restraints, which he was diligently working to slip off of his legs, and the caged back passenger compartment of the patrol car.

My partner immediately pulled over onto the side of the service road. The third officer met us there, because she had heard the radio transmission, and she knew we were in for a challenge. We were going to have to open the door and try to regain control of this kid, and now we were closer to the danger of speeding cars on the freeway. He still had both pairs of the handcuffs hanging from one of his wrists, which rendered him extremely dangerous to all involved. Even so, we had to approach him and stop him before anyone was hurt.

The officer who had been driving entered through the driver's side back door and the other two of us opened the passenger side back door to subdue this young man. He began thrashing about, fighting, wriggling, spitting, and slinging the cuffs. It became clear that there were few options available to subdue him safely. As a result, I pulled out my pepper spray and doused the kid in the face. This seemed to agitate him even more at first, but after about fifteen seconds, he began to writhe in misery. At this point, we were able to handcuff him again with both pair of cuffs. We reconnected the leg restraints, and belted the kid back into the seat. The back seat was not a very big area, especially considering the plastic cage that was separating it from the front half of the car. Consequently, the pepper spray could not disperse because it did not have anywhere to go. My assist officer got a pretty hefty dose of the spray, himself.

Not only had it become necessary to stop on the side of the road and re-restrain our passenger, now my assist officer was rendered unable to drive because of the remnant of the pepper spray in the back of the car. The third officer would now have to drive his car while he sat in the back seat next to the suspect on the ride to the detention center. This would also ensure that the suspect did not escape again, or cause any damage to the vehicle during the transport. I would still be following in my own car. The other officer had to park her vehicle in a nearby parking lot and leave it there temporarily.

This had been a rather exhausting episode, and as I followed my partners to our destination, I realized I was winded, perspiring heavily, and still reeling from the adrenaline rush. Despite struggling with four or five adults, however, this kid never got winded and never lost any of his ability to fight. He never ran out of energy the entire time we had wrestled with him. I truly believed (and still do believe) that he was demon possessed. He yelled with a shrilling and raspy yell, his eyes looked empty and dead inside. He reacted with such violence to even being touched by anyone who was trying to deal with him that I was certain he had some type of superhuman strength, and it wasn't being used for good! I was driving, thinking, and trying to regain my breath. Ultimately, I was able to gain my second wind as I followed my partners.

This was made possible by the sight of my first assist officer, who was sitting on the left passenger side of the back seat next to the student. The kid was still writhing around in discomfort from the stinging pepper spray. However, my partner had the window rolled down, and for a moment, he was riding down the freeway with his head sticking out of the car, like a happy dog riding along with his master. The pepper spray was affecting him almost as badly as it affected the suspect. He was trying to air out the car and relieve some of the stinging from his eyes during the ride. Driving behind him allowed me to see the unusual silhouette of his head sticking out of the window. This was quite an amusing sight. I began to laugh uncontrollably because considering what we had all just experienced, it was one of the funniest things I had ever seen. Although his misery was by no means funny, the view from my vantage point was hilarious. This comic relief seemed to remove the sting from all of the paperwork we would be completing during the next several hours.

# Chapter Fourteen
## Tools of the Trade

### Shotgun Burglary

Throughout my career and even after I retired, whenever anyone finds out that I was a police officer, one of the first questions they ask is, "Have you ever shot anyone?" Well, I never had the unfortunate occasion to shoot at a suspect during my career. Thankfully, I have also never been shot *at*. However, this story portrays the time when I was closest I have ever been to pulling that trigger out of fear for my life.

While I was working patrol one midnight shift at about 3:00 a.m., I received an alarm call in the 2800 block of Hemphill Street. No other officers were available to assist at the time. It was a boarding house with a business office on the lower level. The office was supposed to be locked, and none of the residents were granted access during the overnight hours. This call was in my normal patrol district on the south side, where I felt comfortable. I told the dispatcher I would take this call alone and advise if I needed an assist when I got there.

While I was en route, a concerned citizen reported seeing three or four teenaged males running out of the front door, one carrying a shotgun. I was still a few blocks away, but I knew that I now had a burglary instead of just an alarm. Because the caller reported the teens running from the business, I felt pretty comfortable approaching the scene. It is rare for criminals to hang around after the alarm has sounded.

Upon my arrival, I saw that the door was closed. I stepped up onto the porch to investigate and found that the door was unlocked. I shined my flashlight around to see if there was anyone lurking inside. I could see no one, and the alarm was shrieking so loudly that I couldn't hear myself think, either. I could see that even though the door was now closed, it had been forced open. There were shards of wood split away from the door facing. The owner definitely needed to come out to the scene to secure this door.

I returned to my vehicle and acquired a phone number from dispatch to contact the owner. This was in 1993 when cell phones were not common. As a result, I had to drive down the street to a convenience store to use the phone and attempt contact. The store was only four blocks from my call. I tried the contact number from the convenience store, but no one answered. I figured I would return to the scene and try to wake one of the residents. Maybe they could help me locate the owner.

When I pulled back up to the building, I failed to follow standard officer safety protocol. Because I had been to this scene just a few moments before, and found no one, I considered it safe. I pulled right up into the driveway, right in front of the office. I immediately noticed that there were lights on in the business office that had been burglarized. I thought to myself, "The owner couldn't have gotten here this quickly." Then I thought again, "Wait a minute – I didn't make any contact with the owner. There is no car here. Who is in there?"

At precisely the time I realized that things were not quite right, I noticed a gap appear in the blinds that were covering the window from the inside. I saw the shadowy figure of a person looking out from behind the closed blinds. Suddenly, the lights went out in the room. I froze in terror. The burglars had returned to finish their work. I remembered the earlier report of a shot gun being wielded in the call details. I got out of my car, un-holstered my weapon and approached the building. There were two concrete pillars at the foot of the stairs leading up to the porch. I hunched behind one of them, with my pistol ready, pointed at the doorway. My .357 magnum would not compete with a shotgun. I was trying to find the most solid cover, and this concrete block suited me.

I pushed the orange "emergency status" button on my radio. This clears the radio airways so that officers in dire situations can broadcast necessary information without interruption. I hastily informed the dispatcher that I had returned to the scene and had suspects inside the building at my location. I also told her that there were probably three of them, and one of them may have a shotgun. I thought my transmissions were being heard by all of my fellow officers on my channel. However, I noticed an eerie silence on the radio. Usually when an officer calls for help, everyone in the vicinity jumps on the air to let you know they are on the way to help. I was mortified that no one was answering me. Finally, I heard the lone voice of a different dispatcher. She called my unit and I answered, still hunched behind this concrete pillar, still trying to hold at least three burglars at bay, alone.

She told me that I had been sent to a default channel, and that she would relay information to my original patrol channel. I was confused, because this had never happened before. I later learned that with that particular radio program, when an officer pushed the emergency status button it disabled any ability to broadcast from that radio until the officer turned the radio off, and then back on again. No one had ever told me this. Now I was in an emergency situation, and had no way to communicate with the officers who were in route to help me. Instead, I was on a different channel where I couldn't hear them and vice versa.

Thankfully I could hear sirens approaching in the distance, and even the Air One helicopter. However, about that time, I noticed the door to the building cracked open, and then slam shut again. I could tell the suspects inside were preparing to bolt. I could not do a whole lot to confront them, considering that they potentially had a shotgun and I had a mere Smith and Wesson six-shot revolver.

I was breathing heavily, and my heart was beating so fast and hard I could feel it through my bulletproof vest. I could hear the helicopter coming closer, but could not really tell if the thumping sound was more from the helicopter, or from my own heartbeat. Unexpectedly, the door to the business office flew open and three bodies ran towards me. I had my finger on the trigger of my pistol, pulling tension. It would not take much for me to fire my weapon. This was the closest I ever came to shooting someone. These guys had to pass within feet of me in order to exit the porch. They ran down the stairs, in a blitz, but I had tunnel vision as I honed in on the shotgun being toted by one of them. When I saw the shotgun, I had to orient myself to decide if it was being held in a manner from which it could be fired, or if it was being simply carried out of the building. By the time I determined that it was just being carried, the three suspects had made it around to the side of the building and were running behind it.

As I relayed all of this information to the dispatcher on my desolate emergency channel, she relayed it to other officers. Unfortunately, crucial time was lost during this process. I ran around the corner in an attempt to catch any the suspects, at least trying to keep a visual on them so I could direct the establishment of a perimeter. The suspects split up in the alley with one running south and the other two running north. In a matter of seconds they were out of sight; I had lost all three of them. Ironically, just about the time all three suspects left my sight, the cavalry showed up. The helicopter was overhead with a spotlight, and patrol vehicles showed up in force. It didn't matter, now, though. It was too late, and the three suspects were probably home by now, surveying all the stolen goods they had heisted from the business.

Although I was disgusted that I had allowed three burglars cornered in a building to get away, I was also glad that I had taken cover. Without assistance it would not have been wise for me to approach the suspects, especially in light of the fact I was out-gunned. I will never forget the sheer terror I felt as I stood outside that building, taking cover behind that concrete pillar. Cars passed by on Hemphill Street having no clue that a shotgun blast might spray out of the doorway at any given moment. It is during times like this that I felt an amplified recognition of God's presence as my protector. Even though I was afraid, I had been guided into the best course of action, and was safe. Even though I felt completely abandoned by those around me (because of the radio issue) I was never apart from the ever encompassing embrace of the Lord. I am so thankful for the assurance that I never had to face a single dangerous or frightening situation alone. In God's Word He tells me, "I will never leave thee, nor forsake thee." (Hebrews 13:5b) This is one of my favorite truths from Scripture because I can take comfort in the knowledge that God shows His continuously unwavering concern for each one of us.

I was glad when I realized that this ordeal was finally over. I discussed with my supervisors the problems with the radio. I was furious that the system that was supposed to help officers actually put me in more danger, and left me hanging without communication.

Because of all the commotion, residents from the upstairs boarding units began to file down to see what was going on. We contacted the owner to request his presence to survey the damage. When he arrived, I told him that I had almost shot one of the suspects because they had run past me with a shotgun. He looked at me with an astounded gaze and immediately went to a nearby closet. He opened the door and became distraught because his antique shotgun was missing. It had been locked in that closet, and the suspects had taken it. He advised me that it was old and rusty, and that it was not loaded. That suspect did not realize how close he had been to being shot for simply carrying an old, rusty, unloaded shotgun out of that building.

## Parting the Pioneer Sea

During the last two years of my career, while a member of the School Security Initiative, I was assigned to W.E. Boswell High School (home of the Pioneers) in north Fort Worth. The Eagle Mountain-Saginaw Independent School District is undoubtedly one of the best districts in the area, and in my opinion, Boswell High School is the crown jewel to the community. I was privileged to hold the position of School Resource Officer there as the capstone to my police experience.

Despite the bliss of having been assigned to such an amazing campus, it quickly became clear that even the very best of schools have issues when almost two-thousand teenagers are pooled into one place, five days a week, for nine months. There is inevitable adolescent chemistry that occasionally leads to dissention in the ranks. At the time, these instances were substantially less frequent at Boswell than at other area schools. Even so, they still existed. On one day when that adolescent chemistry yielded one of those explosive reactions, I found myself having to resort to drastic measures for the safety of my students.

Boswell's campus is reminiscent of a college campus, having buildings set apart and outdoor walkways leading from one academic building to another. On this particular day, a relatively violent fight involving several male and female students developed in one of the outdoor walkways. I could tell there was a problem at first by observing the large number of students running during passing period. Students aren't usually that anxious to get to class. However, when there is a fight, they have to be right in the middle of it, pronto. Next, my hunch was confirmed when I began to hear a loud and vigorous chanting of the words, "fight, fight, fight" despite the fact that we weren't in the middle of a football pep-rally, and those voices definitely weren't from the cheerleaders. I knew I had to break this fight apart as soon as possible, and it was clear that the crowd was growing exponentially, which would make it nearly impossible for me to gain access to the students.

Teenagers love to watch scuffles, which from time to time can serve as a pretty good form of free entertainment for a couple of minutes between classes. It doesn't take more than one or two minutes of fighting to give young teenagers enough material to discuss for a week. As a result, when these fights break out, the students do not want to allow the adults access to the fight to break it up. This results in ploys on their part to foil the progress of administrators and police officers. One of the most popular tactics for keeping the violence at a peak in the designated fight area is for the surrounding students to lock arms and create a human boxing ring by linking a circle of students around the entertainment venue.

During this fight, I witnessed a female student knocked to the ground on the concrete walkway. The other students continued fighting, and the crowd was focused on them, not on the girl who was on the ground. She wasn't moving, and I was not sure how badly she had been hurt. Furthermore, I was concerned that the other students, oblivious to anything but the main-event, would trample this student as the fight progressed and fluidly moved down the walkway. I had to make a quick decision that would move these students out of my way. I could not hesitate, so I decided to use my Taser. As per regulations, I warned the students that they needed to move. I yelled, "Police! Move! Get out of the way!" This, of course, fell upon deaf ears for two reasons. First of all, the chanting was nearly deafening. Secondly, those who were close enough to recognize me did not want to allow me to get through and break up the fight.

I had never used my Taser before today. This weapon would emit an attention-getting electric charge of voltage. The affect was a temporary disability of muscle function when the device was deployed and made contact with the subject. Officers who carried a Taser were required to complete an extensive training program which provided all of the appropriate protocol and outlined the circumstances that were appropriate for using this weapon. This situation was a textbook example of how the Taser could effectively regain control in a volatile situation.

I removed my Taser from its holster. Next, I removed the cartridge that was designed to propel two wires with prongs into the clothing or flesh of a suspect. Customarily, when an officer would use the Taser, it was to subdue one subject who was out of control. The prongs would shoot out of the device, connecting to the clothing or the skin of the subject, causing the voltage to stun muscle movement for five seconds. This use of the Taser prongs in this particular situation was not going to be helpful to me. However, without the cartridge, the Taser could be used as a prod. If needed, I could touch the shoulder of any student who blocked my way, and they would immediately fall away from the interlocked ring that hindered my progress. I quickly found that it would not be necessary for me to touch anyone with the device. After I checked to make sure the cartridge was removed I held the Taser up over my head and yelled, "Taser, Taser, Taser!" the warning which is protocol before deploying the device.

Several students heard me and saw the Taser up over my head in the air. They yelled expletives and began to back away quickly. Then, when I pulled the trigger activating a five-second cycling of the device, it emitted a very loud, sharp crackling sound. The students nearby jumped about two feet up in the air, and began scampering away, vacating the area. Immediately, there was a parting of these students, which made a clear path between me and the girl who was lying on the ground. There were a couple of teachers with me, and one of them attended to the girl, helping her up and to the nurse's office. I moved to the students who were still fighting and pulled one apart from the other. Another teacher pulled one of the other students away. It was then that I was finally able to place cuffs on both students, and the fight was finally over. All it took was a five-second cycling of the crackling Taser to part the Pioneer Sea. Luckily, no one was harmed by the device, and the students who were fighting were stopped before anyone else could sustain injury. Mission accomplished.

## Un-Guarded Mishap

The Taser is just one of several non-lethal weapons police officers have at their disposal in the midst of a crisis situation. Pepper-spray is another very effective tool for stopping most suspects when compliance is challenged. I have used my pepper spray several times during my career, but two times in particular stand out in my mind when I recall those struggles.

The first occasion was when I was assigned to a guard detail once at John Peter Smith Hospital. The person I was guarding was a female who had attempted suicide. She was handcuffed to her bed, and was awake. About halfway through my two-hour assignment with her, she summonsed me to her bedside and asked me if she could go to the restroom. She was under the influence of some type of drug that she had ingested in a large quantity. Always leery of any request that involved removing handcuffs, I asked for a medical assistant to accompany both of us to the restroom. The suspect became agitated, asking, "What do you think I am going to do, run away? I can barely walk!"

I followed her as she hobbled to the restroom nearby with the assistance of the nurse. She entered the tiny single bathroom and the nurse stood by with the door ajar to avoid a lock-in situation. I stood a few feet away where I could hear the female but not intrude on her privacy as she used the facilities. After all, she was not a criminal (yet). She was only under care for a suicide attempt. She had appeared compliant in every way up to this point, and was literally hobbling and dragging her feet when we traveled the few feet from her bed to the restroom.

Suddenly, the door flung open. The suspect pushed the nurse aside and took off running down the hallway like an Olympic sprinter. I was close but must admit she caught me off guard. As a result, she actually got a few steps ahead of me before I realized what was happening. I began chasing her down the shiny white-tiled hospital hallway, just like one might imagine seeing in a scene from a movie.

She was a very cunning young lady. Her earlier groggy, hobbling walk and her seemingly compliant behavior was part of her plan. She intended to appear somewhat disabled so she could attempt to escape from the hospital. Even so, I was not under the influence of an overdose of drugs, so I was able to catch up with her very quickly, and when I did, we both went to the floor. We scuffled for a few seconds before I realized that this young lady was a fighter. She pulled the hair clip from behind my head and caused my long hair to fall hanging around my collar. That was an opportunity for her to strike in a big way. She grabbed a handful of my hair and began pulling it.

Before the hair-pulling episode began, our scuffle had not been a volatile situation. It was simply a minor inconvenience and a routine attempt to subdue an unruly subject. Now, however, she resorted to an offensive fighting stance, where before she had simply been defending herself from being placed in handcuffs. It became clear that as she was pulling clumps of my hair downward towards the floor that I was actually in danger. This woman had an adrenaline rush that rendered her some type of superhuman strength.

I unsnapped my pepper-spray canister from its holster and released a squirt of the blazing, hot, stinging mist right into her face. I was able to get the cuffs onto the suspect almost immediately after using the spray, and it was a good thing. I had not been able to see the small crowd of hospital personnel gathering around us as she and I had struggled in the hallway. They were surrounding us, and there was no way this suspect could have escaped. However, while I was tumbling around with her on the ground with my hair being pulled and yanked around, it was impossible for me to know this. When the remnant mist of the pepper spray began to emanate throughout the hallway, about ten or twelve of the surrounding nurses and assistants began to cough and hack. I was teary-eyed, myself, because in the enclosed environment, the pepper spray tends to affect anyone within a twenty-yard radius.

The lead nurse became enraged with me, and yelled loudly, "Don't you know better than to use that stuff in here! This is a hospital! We will never clear this out of here!" She was livid, and I had no reply for her other than to re-focus my attention on the suspect and ask the nurses where they wanted to take her to rinse her eyes out. I still stand by my decision to use the pepper-spray. The other option was my expandable baton, because this was several years before my Taser was issued. The baton would have undoubtedly caused severe injury to the suspect, because she was fighting me so violently, I would have had to hit her very hard several times to gain compliance. This did not seem to be the best course of action at the time, in my opinion. Even so, I single-handedly cleared out the secondary trauma wing of the hospital that night, and learned a lesson about suicidal suspects.

## Airing-Out Differences

The second time the use of pepper-spray angered a building-full of people was when I worked at my alternative ninth grade high school campus. During passing period one day, there was a pretty intense fight between two teen-aged boys in the hallway outside my office. I was standing nearby with a fellow officer who was visiting my campus, but who was unfamiliar with the spontaneous violence which routinely erupted in the hallways. As a result, when she observed the fighting, she reacted differently than I normally would have. She and I both broke through the crowd and tried to each grab a student and separate them. These guys were big, angry and adrenalized from fighting. Consequently, they did not respond to us, and actually drug us both along with them as they continued throwing punches.

My colleague had enough, and quickly pulled her pepper-spray out. She pointed it right at the upper body area of both boys and sprayed it. The students who had gathered to watch began coughing and hacking. The two fighting students began gagging. So did I. So did my colleague. So did the teachers and the students in the classrooms nearby. The spray had entered the ventilation system and was being dispersed to the classrooms that were closest to the fight.

We subdued the two students and placed them in cuffs. Then we relocated them to my office to de-escalate the situation. Even so, several other students and teachers were affected by the harsh and potent spray. The teacher whose room was nearest my office came to me immediately and yelled at me. It sounded very familiar. "Did you have to do that in here? Don't you realize this is a school? This will be in the air for the rest of the day!" I'm telling you, it sounded familiar.

The only answer I had for this teacher was "I'm sorry." I actually *was* regretful for the inconvenience because I worked in this school every day and I had a positive rapport with the staff. This teacher was one of my favorites, and I felt somewhat badly that the incident had upset her so much.

Ultimately, however, it boiled down to the fact that my colleague had chosen to use her pepper spray to diffuse a volatile situation. I was not going to pass the buck and place blame on her. She did what she thought needed to be done. The fight ended, and some people cried about it for awhile. That's that. After all, as officers who were in the midst of the fight, we had actually received a bigger dose than anyone else other than the participants. I had little sympathy for the students who were gathered around in a circle egging it on. The students at this school fought rather often. However, on this day, they learned that fighting was not so cool after all - and neither was being a spectator.

## A Case for the Taser
*[This story depicts violence]*

During the earlier years of my career when I still worked midnight shift patrol on the south side, my partner and I were dispatched to a man who was sleeping in his truck. Upon our arrival, we observed the truck which appeared to have been driven up to the edge of the roadway, coming to rest perpendicular to the curb. The engine was running, and the driver was passed out in the driver's seat. He was clearly extremely intoxicated because the odor of alcohol was very apparent, and his wet jeans indicated that he had urinated on himself.

This was not an uncommon occurrence for this part of town. After all, it was about three blocks from where I had been involved in my serious crash just months before, wherein the drunk driver had hit my patrol vehicle while his truck was travelling about 60 mph. The area was speckled with dance clubs and corner bars and plenty of working-class folks who frequented them. As a result, intoxicated drivers were rampant.

I realized that I would have to reach across the man's body to turn off the ignition. I did so, and removed the key. I also tried to put the truck in park, but I realized that I would be unable to depress the brake. The man still had his foot on the gas pedal, so I abandoned that idea. Even so, we had to wake up this man and get his vehicle out of the middle of the road before another drunk hit it.

Our suspect was a very small man, about 5'4" and looked to weigh about 140 pounds. He was passed out, cold, and did not respond to my attempts to address him. He was Latino, so we decided that perhaps he did not understand English. Our next course of action was to gently shake his left shoulder in a further attempt to wake him. This did not work, either.

Next, we decided to try a harmless but painful technique that works to wake up almost anyone, no matter how sound asleep they might be. This technique is accomplished by taking a pen or pencil and holding it next to the fingernail of a subject. Pressure is then applied to the writing utensil and, when done properly, it sends a jolt of pain through the body that violently wakes the senses. I learned this technique when I was an

Emergency Medical Technician, and it never failed me, unless the person on whom I attempted it was actually dead.

I grabbed hold of the passed-out driver's left hand and arranged my pen as described. Then, I applied the pressure. This tiny little man who was in the third stage of dreamland opened his eyes and sat straight up in the seat. He had been jolted awake by the technique, just as we had hoped. However, he was now very angry and appeared to be scared, as well, seeing two uniformed police officers in his face.

He grabbed hold of my right arm and used me as leverage to exit his truck. He was a bit wobbly, but he moved pretty quickly. I was glad he was getting out of the truck, because I had to cuff him and take him to the "detox" tank at the jail for his public intoxication, anyway. It became clear really quickly that this man did not speak English. He began slurring a string of words in Spanish. Neither my partner nor I could understand him. As we attempted to calm him, he became more and more agitated. Again, this was not an uncommon occurrence and unfortunately, there was not an overabundance of Spanish-speaking officers available nearby at the time to translate. I always relied on the staff at the jail to explain the details about the "detox," and how the suspect could retrieve his car from the auto pound when he was released. This worked most of the time. It wouldn't work tonight.

My partner grabbed the keys and leaned into the truck to put it into park. During this time, I was about ten feet away, alone with the suspect who became angered by the idea of my partner entering his truck. He began struggling with me and gained a seemingly super-human strength boosted by his fear and adrenaline. He was intoxicated, but apparently he was accustomed to fighting. As my partner was still in the truck trying to secure it, the man caught me off guard with his power. Yes, he was a small, drunk man, and he was strong. It happens. I have already explained that I was not the most skilled in the fighting department. Even so, I was surprised that this small man suddenly became so violent. I was leaning into him in a very unstable position. All the while I was trying to evaluate a strategy to gain control over him.

Before I could exact a tactical advantage, he grabbed my arm and slung me, headfirst into the concrete sidewalk. I saw those little tweeting birds that are often portrayed in cartoons. I was knocked into a state of momentary confusion. We both went to the ground and continued to scuffle. I was now stunned and recovering from a pretty hard blow to my head, after having hit the ground with it. The suspect skillfully grabbed for my gun. As I attempted to defend my weapon with one hand, I was leaning up on the other. The suspect continued using both of his hands to try and peel mine away. He was trying enthusiastically to get to my pistol. I was feeling somewhat weak and groggy, but I knew this was one of those situations where I had to fight with every cell in my being, or my partner and I would *both* be in danger.

I was exhausted, but I kept fighting, and I yelled for my partner to help me. This had all happened so fast that he did not realize what was going on until I was on the ground fighting to maintain control of my pistol. He jumped quickly into action, though, and took care of business. He grabbed his expandable baton and began yelling the protocol warnings, "Stop fighting. Stop fighting." The man continued diligently trying to peel my tired hands away from my holster snap. My partner began striking the man methodically with the baton as we are trained to do, on the arms and on the side of his torso, while still yelling warnings. The man barely reacted to the pain of the blows. Actually, they only made him angrier. As a result, he flung himself upward to face-off with my partner. He did this at precisely the same time my partner was swinging a blow to his arm with the baton. The baton made contact with the back of the suspect's head, and he fell forward, completely unconscious from that powerful strike. He hit the ground, face-first, and did not move.

Although I was thankful for being out of danger, my partner was now mortified. He looked at me and said, "Kelly! I think I killed him!" He was genuinely worried that this man was dead. I, however, redirected my partner into reality by reminding him that the man was trying to get my gun. After all, he wasn't planning on selling it at the pawn shop. If he would have gained control of it, there is no telling what could have happened to either of us.

I was relieved because I was exhausted and had been running out of strength to maintain control of my gun. A carload of Code Blue "Citizens on Patrol" volunteers had pulled up to the scene and had been watching the entire situation as it unfolded. They witnessed the warnings being yelled, and the strikes being made to the arms and the torso. Then, they witnessed the man jump up right into the swing of my partner's baton, rendering him falling face-first, unconscious, with a huge gash across the back of his skull.

This was another instance where I could clearly see the hand of God at work protecting my partner and me. Not only did He place a force field around us, He also provided the absolute perfect circumstances to ensure our safety. Furthermore, He provided credible witnesses to corroborate the truth. Without them, the situation could very easily have been perceived as one of excessive force or police brutality.

MedStar ambulance personnel arrived to evaluate both the suspect and me. I had a bump on my head and was a little sore, but I was fine. The suspect, however, had to go to the hospital to get several stitches across the back of his scalp. He also sustained a bloody nose and a busted lip from hitting the ground face-first. He was, however, very much alive.

As I mentioned before, it turned out to be a blessing of uncommon significance that the "Citizens on Patrol" volunteers had witnessed the entire event. They were able to provide statements to the Internal Affairs Division that defended any perception of wrongdoing by my partner. Even though he felt a bit of regret for the situation, I have always considered my partner a hero for defending me so well. He has always remembered the sheer terror that came from thinking he had killed a man with his baton. This is why I call this story "A Case for the Taser."

# Chapter Fifteen
## Roadway Risks Realized

Being up on an overpass while traffic is zooming by at upwards of sixty miles per hour is dangerous enough. However, being on the open freeway where vehicles are racing by at near eighty is much, much worse. When officers have to work accidents on the freeway, I am quite positive the risk is higher than that of entering a situation with an armed criminal. At least when an officer is facing an armed criminal, he or she is most likely anticipating volatility. However, while out in the roadway gathering information from a vehicle to complete an accident report, or clearing away a bumper, a wheel, or sharp shards of metal that were impacted off of a vehicle during a crash, an officer can easily become distracted. Often, close calls are reported as officers are barely missed by speeding cars that are oblivious to the danger, despite the emergency flashers and road flares.

## Temper Flare-Up
*[This story contains mildly undesirable language]*

One time very early in my career I was assisting with an accident at I-35W southbound at the Ripy Street exit. Other officers were up ahead of me caring for the victims, but it was obvious that the accident was going to require some lengthy investigation before it could be cleared. As a result, I moved over to my patrol vehicle and lugged out a box of flares. I began cracking them together, setting up a flare line across the outside two lanes to protect the officers up ahead of me. Another officer arrived, who just happened to be from my academy class. He began asking me what he needed to do. I told him I was just going to throw out a quick line of flares and get back in the car.

About that time, my sergeant, whom I had only worked with for about three weeks approached me from the side of the outer freeway median. In a loud, shrill, and extremely angry voice, he began to yell at me, "Get out of the road. You are going to get yourself killed."

I explained to him that I was setting up the flare line. He rebutted, "I said to get out of the road – NOW! This is not a game of hopscotch. People will run over you. I will do the flare line. Get out of here."

When he yelled, the veins began to pop out from his forehead, and he looked rather scary. He was really upset. I was perplexed, because he implied that he must have had a method of setting up a flare line that did not involve getting in the roadway. I knew this would be impossible, but the way he was ranting, I wanted to see him try it. Even so, I would not get to.

"Clear this call now. Get out of here!" Because he was obviously extremely agitated, I quickly followed his order and immediately left the scene. His patrol car was in front of mine, with the emergency flashers on, so I figured he was safe enough. I went down the block into a church parking lot and began to complete the details of the call on my worksheet. I was really disturbed from having been yelled at. This had cropped up completely out of the blue, and I was in a state of shock. I continued working the rest of the busy Saturday night shift when a couple of hours later I heard that gruff, angry voice on the police radio calling my unit.

"Go ahead," I answered.

"54 with me at the sector" This meant that he wanted to meet with me.

"Ten-four, I'm en-route." I headed to the sector, now fearing that for some reason I was about to get a punishment akin to the spankings that I got from my Dad when I was five years old. I was really very nervous in anticipation of this meeting. I dreaded it, and I drove slower than I should have. When I arrived, I went into the sergeant's office. He told me to sit down. I braced for the worst.

"I am sorry I yelled at you out there. It's just that traffic is unforgiving, and I did not want to see one of my new troops get killed. You have got to be more careful out there on that freeway!" I remember the exact words because I can still see his face as he said them. He was apologizing to me for caring about me! He smiled and I felt completely exonerated.

I told him that I understood his concern, and I appreciated it. I just didn't know what I was doing that was so wrong. He then explained to me that from a distance he saw me and the other officer from my class standing in the roadway talking. He did not know the brevity of our exchange, apparently, and thought we were having a lengthy conversation out there on the freeway. When he saw this, he became engulfed with a father-like urgency to protect us by yelling like a madman. He laughed about his temper, and I did too, but only after he laughed first!

Over the years and after his having been promoted to the rank of lieutenant I would see this man in passing from time to time. He would always say, "That's my girl. Have you had a good ass-chewing lately?" We would both chuckle. Then, without fail, he would always feel the need to explain to me again his reason for losing his temper. He was only yelling at me because he did not want me to get hurt or killed. I suppose he felt guilty because he probably never forgot how pitiful I looked that night when he poured his wrath out on me in the middle of the freeway!

## Inches from Disaster

The recollection of events for this segment is really challenging for me, as they will be for any Fort Worth Police Officer who reads it. I could never count the times I have been standing on the side of the roadway with a traffic violator sitting in his or her vehicle, when suddenly, the side-view mirror of a speeding vehicle brushed by behind me at speeds in excess of seventy miles per hour. Even now I can feel the wind generated from the speed of the passing cars as I remember the terror of the closeness of them.

Sometimes those mirrors have passed by within inches of my person, as I have stood out in the roadway doing my job, and it is by the grace of God alone that I have not been hit. These dangerous encounters occurred on a very regular basis in spite of the fact that there was always a patrol vehicle behind the violator, and that patrol vehicle had emergency red and blue, and even amber flashing lights to warn motorists to slow down and avoid the immediate area (at least within a foot) of the officer who is investigating a traffic violation. It would seem that this would happen less at night, when the flashing lights warn anyone with vision from what seems like a mile away, that something is happening up ahead.

However, these warnings don't always connect with drivers out on the roadway during the dark hours, as is evidenced by the number of officers struck by vehicles and killed every year while attempting to execute traffic stops.

## Alan Chick
*[This story contains extremely graphic and disturbing material]*

In the pitch, black, darkness on the rainy Wednesday morning of December 22, 1993, just three days before Christmas, I experienced one of the worst days of my life. This was the morning that a drunk driver would mistakenly perceive the red and blue flashing lights coming from the light bar of one of my colleague's vehicle as an attraction, instead of a warning. His intoxicated and fatigued mind would focus directly upon the strobing illumination as he slammed full-force into Officer Alan Chick at highway speeds, throwing his body up onto and over his speeding vehicle, and back onto the ground, in a near lifeless state.

It was well after 3:30 a.m. when the dark, rain-soaked roadway became a resting place for the broken body of a hero. Officer Chick was helping a stranded motorist who was stalled on Interstate 20, eastbound near the Oak Grove Road underpass. This was a dangerous area at night, and the female driver and her tired passenger were in need of a jump-start for the sluggish battery in the stalled truck. Another car occupied by two men had just stopped on the side of the road with the woman, but instead of helping her, they scared her to death. She had asked them to leave and began screaming for help.

Very shortly afterward, she was greeted by Officer Chick, who came to the rescue, parking his patrol vehicle as he did hundreds of times before, angled off to the side of the roadway, with all flashing emergency lights activated. After finding out that she needed her battery charged, Officer Chick knew he would have to move his vehicle around in front of the woman's truck in order to connect the jumper cables. Even so, the flashing lights were illuminating the night sky, leaving no doubt that any vehicles approaching the area should have done so with caution.

Via radio transmission, Officer Chick asked me to stop the vehicle that had just left the scene, to make sure they had not been attempting to harm the stranded female. As a result, I moved on ahead, following that car.

I stopped it and spoke with its occupants. I was able to determine that the men had actually been trying to help the woman, and had just scared her by approaching her vehicle as she sat, already nervous from having car trouble. I gathered their names and information, and sent them on their way. As I began to return to the scene and assist Officer Chick, he was handing the woman her jumper cables back through the driver's side window.

Then the unthinkable happened. The woman watched helplessly as Officer Chick turned his attention away from her, and towards the speeding deadly weapon which was heading right for him. She watched as the car hit the officer, and saw the entire, tragic, event take place, right in front of her. The next thing any on duty officers knew, we all heard the shrilling, screaming voice of a woman on a police radio.

Her unintelligible screaming was dotted sporadically with words that all officers on the channel could hear. Within seconds, we had deciphered the phrases and words that made up the chilling plea, "Help! This officer has been hit! We need help, this officer is down! Get us some help!"

I knew, immediately for whom she was yelling. The gut-instinct feeling set me into a state of adrenaline fueled flight back to the scene of that stranded motorist. I notified the dispatcher that I thought the woman was calling out from Officer Chick's location, and that she was using his radio.

I had been right there near the scene with Officer Chick just moments before this life-changing crash occurred. How could this happen? One second, one split-second he was doing his job, and the very next, he lay near death in a fetal position, posturing, losing blood, on the hard, wet road.

When I arrived back to the scene, I actually did not drive all the way back to it. Instead, because I was returning westbound from having stopped that possible suspect vehicle, I pulled up to the Oak Grove exit on the westbound side of the road. I could see the woman jumping around frantically, and could still hear her yelling on the radio. I exited my patrol vehicle, and without a memory of even looking into the freeway, I crossed eight lanes, jumping the concrete median that separated the highway. I saw the woman standing over Officer Chick, crying uncontrollably. The person who had been in need of assistance from this man now became a hero to him by her quick thinking. She had witnessed (and had been involved in) the crash as the suspect scraped along the vehicles parked there, scooping up Officer Chick along the way. She immediately got out of her truck and approached Officer Chick to try and help him as he lay there, gravely injured. The only thing she knew to do was to use his radio to call for help. She summonsed help, and did so bravely, especially considering what she had just experienced.

Upon my arrival back to that scene, I confirmed that Officer Chick had indeed been hit by a car. I called for an ambulance, for supervisors, more assist officers, and even for Care-flight. All the time, the suspect was about fifty yards ahead of the mangled mess, where his car had come to rest. He had not yet exited the damaged vehicle. I could see the silhouette of his body in the driver's seat. I then re-focused my attention on the safety and care of Officer Chick. Even so, it should be noted, that this man had been arrested thirteen previous times for DWI, and convicted eight times. Yet, with our justice system as it is, he was still able to drive that night, and was again, intoxicated.

While waiting for help to arrive, I remember attending to Officer Chick as he lay there, unconscious, only slightly moving as blood poured from his face. I checked his pulse, which was weak, but present. I held his neck still until his breathing became heavy and he began violently gurgling blood. It became necessary for me to attempt to clear his airway by scooping gushing blood and loosened teeth out from the inside of his mouth with my bare hands. I will never forget the feeling of his warm blood on my hands and of his teeth scraping across my fingers. He was sucking air and blood, causing a raspy sound as he tried to inhale, then a bubbling sound as he exhaled, choking laboriously. Even so, he was still alive, at least for the present time.

Recalling the event, I can vividly remember squeezing his limp hand, telling him, "We are here. We are getting you help. It is going to be okay. Just hold on." Our police helicopter was out flying that morning, and I remember it landing in the roadway, just yards away from us. Then, as other officers began to arrive and saw me there kneeling on the road with Officer Chick, they approached, mortified. I was holding his hand, and I thought I could feel him gripping it back. I was talking to him, not sure if he could hear me, still telling him that we were working to get him help.

When the other officers did arrive on the scene, I became overwhelmed with the situation. Knowing now that other officers were on hand to assist, I lost my composure and began to cry. Then I began to yell. I don't remember exactly what all I yelled, but I remember yelling. I do think I yelled for the ambulance to hurry up. It was still not there. It seemed like it had been an hour, but it had only been minutes.

One of my fellow officers, a veteran of many years, arrived and was attempting to restore order to this extremely chaotic situation. He stood me up and walked me away, trying to remove me from the area. He placed me in a patrol car and told me that I needed to calm down and stay in the car. He did so in a stern, condescending manner, which made me very angry. I remember thinking at the time that he made me feel like a little five-year old child who had just witnessed something off limits. I mistakenly felt as if he were belittling me. I ignored him and exited the vehicle so that I could return to Officer Chick. I had promised Alan as I knelt beside him that I would not leave him until the medical help arrived. This other officer did not know that, and it probably wouldn't have mattered considering how I was acting. However, despite his frustration with me, I just stayed there with Alan, crying and holding his hand until the paramedics arrived.

I know that the other officer was going through emotional trauma, too, and was simply trying to remove me from the area because I was not helping anymore. He was a very good friend and a long time colleague of Officer Chick. When I look back on that morning I feel very badly for having acted so out-of-control at the time. This officer should not have had to address my behavior when there were other important tasks that needed to be tended. Everyone on the scene was upset and stressed out. Everyone was trying to get help for Alan and also trying to secure the suspect who had caused all of this tragic mess, while working to avoid another collision with the traffic which was approaching the scene in the rain. Unfortunately, I had become a hindrance. This veteran officer was obviously horror-struck, as well, but he was able to maintain his composure because of his maturity and his professionalism.

Even so, he could not have realized what this had been like for me, as I had just been scooping teeth and blood out of Alan's mouth. I am certain that I maintained my professionalism on that scene *until other officers and medical personnel were there to take over.* However, as soon as I felt that there was enough help there to secure the situation, I know I let myself go into a state of numbness and "auto-pilot." That was accompanied by my emotional outburst of crying and yelling. Consequently I began to verbally express the horror that we were all living at the moment. Quite frankly, I don't remember what else happened there.

The ambulance was taking so long to arrive that the Air-One crew considered loading Officer Chick in it and flying him to the hospital. Finally, however, the MedStar ambulance arrived and the professional medical assistance Alan needed was there. They carefully attended to him, quickly loaded him onto the truck, and sped away with flashing lights and sirens to John Peter Smith Hospital. I vaguely remember maneuvering back across the eight lanes of traffic, getting in my car, and following the ambulance to the hospital. However, if someone told me that I didn't drive that morning, they may be right. I only know for certain that I eventually ended up at the hospital and waited helplessly as the medical staff worked tirelessly to evaluate the extent of injury to my fellow officer and friend.

Several officers began to gather in the emergency room at the hospital. I was numb, and don't remember many specific details about that morning. The only thing I do remember clearly was the conversation Alan and I had just before his last call. He was telling me that he had most of his Christmas shopping done, all except one last gift for his daughter. He wanted to buy her a little sweat suit because she had mentioned that she wanted one. He was planning to go shopping later that day to buy this last-minute gift for his little girl. As I was sitting there, thinking about Alan's two very small children, I became heartbroken and angry. This daughter and son were at home sleeping, eagerly awaiting the holidays with their Daddy. They had no idea that while they peacefully slept, the decision an intoxicated criminal, who had no regard for human life had made, had forever changed their lives. To further enhance my despair, I knew that officers had been dispatched to Alan's home to inform his wife of this tragic crash. She would be learning any minute now that her husband may never come home again. That is a knock on the door that every officer's family dreads, and prays never happens. I kept imagining what that might be like in my mind, over and over.

It became clear within the next two days that Officer Chick's injuries were irreversible, barring a miracle. He had swelling in his brain, internal injuries and massive trauma to his entire body that were just too much for any earthly human shell to combat. Even so, it was not emotionally possible for his family to remove his life support on Christmas Eve or Christmas Day. As a result, they waited until the holiday was officially over. On December 26, 1993, the family reluctantly made the difficult decision to remove Alan from life support. He died within minutes. Even though he had been essentially brain-dead since soon after the initial impact, this brought a dreadful finality to the situation.

I remember standing by the nurse's station as the life support machines were removed. I was feverishly watching the monitor that reported the sharp spikes on the baseline, each of which represented a heartbeat. As long as I could see those spikes being reported on the screen appearing every fraction of a second, I felt some hope. However, a few short moments after the life-sustaining equipment was removed, the spikes faded into a solid, straight line. At that moment I felt as if I had died too. I was standing against a wall. I remember melting, sliding down the wall, literally, until I was sitting on the floor of the hospital. I wanted to roll up into a ball and disappear. I was devastated. Not only had I lost a friend, but a family had lost a father, husband, brother, and son. The Fort Worth Police Department had lost a friend and an asset to the force, and the world had lost a hero.

Other officers worried about me because of my reaction to this loss. For some reason, my behavior was deemed as excessive. My crying, sadness, grief, and sense of loss were questioned. There was no reason I should have been this upset. This is what I was told. These people did not realize that, as I wrote before, death was a stranger to me up until the past several months. Then, it hit my life with a vengeance because I had dealt with it three times within a calendar year.

The call I detailed earlier where Felicia committed suicide was traumatic for me, as I explained in great depth. She was a stranger, but that experience became very real to me, and the reality of "death" for our earthen, fallen bodies became brutally clear as I watched her family members begin to absorb their indescribable loss. Shortly after that my own father was diagnosed with an aggressive lung cancer. He died very quickly from this cancer in September of 1993, after an eight month, hard-fought battle. That was my Daddy. I was not prepared to handle the loss of my own family member, my own father. This had been the hardest thing I had ever had to face. As a matter of fact, I had been discussing the loss of my father with Alan in the days before his horrible accident.

He was helping me as I tried to deal with the thought of my mother and me spending our first holiday season without my Daddy. We had been spending a lot of time together talking, and his friendship seemed to give me the power and strength to press forward.

Then, in an instant, Alan was gone. Three times I had dealt with traumatic death scenarios, and two of those were people who were important in my everyday life, and both whom I loved dearly. Where in the instruction book for life does it dictate how one is supposed to deal with that much loss and grief appropriately?

As a result of my grieving which was deemed uncommon and excessive by my peers and supervisors, I was taken to a room in the hospital by a psychologist. He shut the door behind us, and asked me to sit down. He then pulled a chair up to the door, and blocked the doorway by sitting in front of it. I was beginning to feel as if I had done something wrong, because I was now being imprisoned. I wanted to be out of that room, where my fellow officers and friends were grieving together and making arrangements for the next couple of days' events. I needed to be a part of that fellowship. Instead, I was held behind the closed door of a stuffy, windowless, hospital counseling room. I was being asked a ton of questions by a man who was convinced I was unfit for duty – all because I was sad that my friend had just died, having his life-support removed the day after Christmas, being essentially killed by a criminal who should have been in prison in the first place. I don't know what he expected me to feel, considering all of these things that had just happened. As a matter of fact, with the benefit of fifteen years to think about it, I still don't really have any idea what others might have expected from me, in light of the situation.

Needless to say, I became extremely agitated in the room, where I was being questioned. I asked the psychologist what it would take for me to be able to get out of the room without being fired or indicted for assault. He condescendingly made me promise to report to him for a few counseling sessions in order to ensure that I was fit for duty. I felt a near hate for him at this point for making me promise to do something I was not willing to do, just to get out of a room at a time when I was very vulnerable. His method was grossly lacking in professionalism, and I will never forget that. As a counseling student today, I know that his understanding of "client location" was absent to a fault.

I was finally released from that room, and a couple of my friends were actually waiting for me outside. They were worried about me (but they did not lock me in a room to check on me). They had waited for me, and asked me how I was doing, considering all that had happened. Through the years, as time passed, I hid my grief, my anger, and my sadness, in order to continue my career. If I didn't hide it, I knew I would be looked upon as unfit - as a liability instead of an asset, by some of my supervisors and colleagues.

As our justice system dictates, it was quite a long time before the trial of the suspect who killed Alan. Consequently, having been the first officer on the scene, I was required to testify at great length during the trial. This was another emotionally difficult situation. My testimony mirrored the events as detailed above. I had to recall all of them and make them public record. Even so, it was worth the pain and the stress just to be a part of the judicial process that would eventually find this man guilty of the intoxication manslaughter. He would finally be confined to prison for the rest of his life, so that others might be safe out on the roads.

After the trial, the emotional trauma (now stirred up once again) continued to nestle itself comfortably into my heart and mind, in places where it would sit and fester for another thirteen years. After all of those years, the pain and trauma of that night has still not left me. As a matter of fact, I never quite realized how calloused the knot of pain in my heart and mind had become, until I was recently required to attend and participate in a series of group therapy sessions as a part of my Counseling Master's Degree at the Southwestern Baptist Theological Seminary. I understood that this mandated therapy was necessary in order that we, as counselors in training, could understand the vulnerable states that our clients would be feeling. As a requirement of group interaction I was asked to choose my own issue to discuss. I have several menial stresses in my life, but nothing seemed to be too pressing. However, the more I thought about what would really be helpful for me to address, the more I felt that hard, calloused knot in my heart bulging out, still causing pain as it tore through my soul.

I was unwittingly placed in the perfect position to face an unresolved issue in my life that needed to be addressed. I did not intend for it to happen, but all paths in my mind led me back to this tragic incident and the loss of my dear friend Alan. The anger, guilt, desperation, loss, grief, and what seemed like hundreds of other emotions came rushing back to me as I worked to express and share these feelings with my group. After an intimately revealing session one night, my counselor recommended that I complete a journal exercise. She felt that if I were to get some of my feelings out on paper, it might help me release some of the negativity associated with this traumatic experience which was obviously still haunting me. She was right! I took that assignment to heart, and God used it as an opportunity to inspire me with a poem that would release me from the anger, guilt and grief of that event. The poem I was led to write some fifteen years after that unremorseful, repeat-offender killed my friend and colleague reads as follows:

### Let it go!
By: Kelly Martin

*Why do you continually drink and then decide to drive?*
*You break the law and act like you're the only one alive.*

*You've met resistance countless times, when the law caught up to you;*
*But your impulses seem to continually thrive, as you do what you've wanted to do.*

*"Nothing applies to me," you say; "I am better than all of the laws."*
*"I will do what I want now and every day;" - "I'm not capable of any flaws."*

*The world is your oyster - you spend every night, looking to find your next high.*
*It doesn't matter what's wrong or what's right; and the victims can't figure out why.*

*What a shame the daughter will not again hear - that Daddy loves her completely;*
*She can only imagine a vision so clear - of his face that once smiled at her sweetly.*

*Never again can the three year old son enjoy the wrestling play,*
*With his Dad as he tackles his "A-number one," on the living room floor every day;*

196

*No more can the magic of holiday time fill the home through the month*
*of December;*
*Because sadness and loss from a hideous crime is all that the loved ones*
*remember;*

*I must do my best to forget all the hate and the judgment I place upon you.*
*I know the Lord will handle your fate, and it's what I'm commanded to do.*

*Forgiveness, though hard, is my duty, you see - I must honor the teachings*
*I've had;*
*For if I remain full of bitter disease, my transgressions will be just as bad;*

*I want to let my light shine bright, but the same story plays out each day;*
*I ask forgiveness both day and night, for returning to my sinful ways.*

*I harbor guilt and even shame, but through God's almighty voice,*
*I recognize we're much the same, and daily we both make a choice.*

*For you it's self-indulgent crimes which lead to tragic endings;*
*For me its anger and hate within that keeps my heart from mending.*

*I live a constant battle fought to turn away from sin,*
*I struggle with the bitter thoughts that break me from within.*

*Who am I to judge the things that haunt you and your selfish heart?*
*When I am doing the very same and have been from the start?*

*Almighty God who gives us grace, He loves us though we fail*
*It is my duty; it is my place, to let His love prevail.*

*So here it is, my final word, which will shed me from binding chains -*
*I forgive, as I'm taught, and replace my despair with praise for my Father,*
*who reigns!*

I reported to therapy with this poem in hand one week after my
journal exercise was assigned. I was given the opportunity to share it with
the other seven members of my group. It was received with open hearts

and open ears as my student-colleagues and my counselor allowed me to read the poem aloud to them. As each word was being read I could feel a layer of the calloused knot in my heart falling away. I was releasing the anger, the grief, the hatred (that I didn't realize I had), and the unfinished business of fifteen years.

The reading of that poem for me was symbolic. It represented my letting go of each of those damaging feelings that had been wrapped in my heart as tightly as a ball of knotted rubber bands. The reading of each line of the poem caused a band to unravel and fall away from the tightly knotted ball. When I was done I was left with what seemed like a harmless pile of weakened bands stretched out of shape and no longer resistant to feeling. The process had softened this spot in my heart so that it could be filled with the love and support from my Lord, and from my fellow group members who genuinely cared about this situation with me. This tightly hardened knot of negative energy was instantaneously annihilated through the work of God's inspiration, in the form of this poem.

Although this crash (I still refuse to call it an accident) resulted in the death of a treasured friend who is still deeply missed, after fifteen years I was finally able to see some of the wisdom of God's plan, which had not been made clear to me for years. I could now recognize that this experience was just another one of many very traumatic events that would equip me for my future in the counseling field. The release of my personal pain through this poem was a gift from God, and affirmation that I was in the right place. My choice to retire early from the Fort Worth Police Department in order to study counseling at this institution was the right decision.

Furthermore, I began to feel confirmation that I should continue writing this book, finish it, and press forward to have it published. The reasons for the existence of this book became threefold: first of all, it is a testimony of Christ's love, which empowered me to overcome numerous adversities in my life; secondly, it is hoped that the circumstances portrayed within will serve as encouragement to others who might be in a similar situation; and most importantly, it is my prayer that some of my readers will come to a personal knowledge of Christ after recognizing the amazing peace that can come from accepting the gift of salvation. For all of these things I give glory to God, and I ultimately count this book as an opportunity to serve Him.

# Chapter Sixteen
## Finding Perfect Peace

How could I write a book detailing the amazing providence of God in my life without sharing Him with those who are reading it? As I said before, I want to communicate the amazing love and peace that comes with the understanding of salvation and the knowledge of Christ. As a result, I am including a step-by-step explanation of how to accept the gift of salvation which God has provided for each and every person who believes in Him. My Scripture references come from the King James Version of God's Word, the Holy Bible.

1.) The first step towards salvation is to understand why it is necessary.

In the very beginning of humanity, during the lifetime of Adam and Eve, sin entered the heart of mankind.

*"3 But the fruit of the tree which is in the midst of the garden, God hath said, Ye shall not eat of it, neither shall ye touch it, lest ye die. 4 And the serpent said unto the woman, Ye shall not surely die: 5 For God doth know that in the day ye eat thereof, then your eyes shall be opened and ye shall be as gods, knowing good and evil. 7 And the eyes of them both were opened and they knew that they wee naked; and they sewed fig leaves together, and made themselves aprons."* (Genesis 3:3-5, 7)

From the time the serpent convinced Eve to eat fruit from the tree God had designated as off-limits, each and every human being since has been born with a sin-nature, or a tendency to sin. Sin is anything that we do that is displeasing to God and against His commands.

According to the Old Testament (the scriptures depicting times before the birth of Christ), the law dictated that perfectly flawless animals had to be slaughtered and sacrificed in order to pay the price for the sins of the people. Even though God was the only one who could make the sacrifice worthy, giving the sacrifice was a sign of obedience and a rightly attitude of God's people who were in need of His forgiveness and grace.

*"27 And if any one of the common people sin through ignorance, while he doeth somewhat against any of the commandments of the Lord concerning things which ought not to be done, and be guilty; 28 Or if his sin, which he hath sinned, come to his knowledge: then he shall bring his offering, a kid of the goats, a female without blemish, for his sin which he hath sinned. 29 And he shall lay his hand upon the head of the sin offering, and slay the sin offering in the place of the burnt offering."* (Leviticus 4:27-29)

It was required by God's law that bloodshed must occur in order to make amends for the sins of the people. This, again, showed a measure of obedience and reverence towards God's sovereignty (power and authority) above humans, as our Creator.

*"11 For the life of the flesh is in the blood: and I have given it to you upon the altar to make an atonement for your souls: for it is the blood that maketh an atonement for the soul."* (Leviticus 17:11)

The birth of Jesus Christ was anticipated and predicted in the Old Testament. The people waited for their promised deliverer, the Messiah, a hope that would be fulfilled when Christ was born. The following verse shows how the prophet Isaiah looked forward to Christ's birth:

*"6 For unto us a child is born, unto us a son is given: and the government shall be upon his shoulder: and his name shall be called Wonderful, Counseller, The mighty God, The everlasting Father, The Prince of Peace."* (Isaiah 9:6)

This prophetic statement was later fulfilled, and detailed in the New Testament (the later scriptures that depict times during and after the birth of Christ). The following verse shows Luke's account of Christ's birth:

> *"11 For unto you is born this day in the city of David a Saviour, which is Christ the Lord. And this shall be a sign into you; Ye shall find the babe wrapped in swaddling clothes, lying in a manger."* (Luke 2:11-12)

After Jesus was born, He grew up to be the only person who ever lived a life without sin. From the very moment of His birth, He knew that His destiny was to die for the sins of all of humanity. Christ's life is symbolic, and parallels the perfectly flawless animal that was required as a blood sacrifice in the times depicted in Old Testament scriptures.

> *"21 For even hereunto were ye called: because Christ also suffered for us, leaving us an example, that ye should follow his steps: 22 Who did no sin, neither was guile found in his mouth:"* (1 Peter 2:21-22)

Without that sacrifice, we would have death and eternal separation from God. We would not have a way to pay for our sins. God will accept nothing less than perfection, and we are not capable of that perfection. With the sacrifice of Christ, however, it is possible for us to have that fellowship with God, and eternal life in heaven.

> *"For the wages of sin is death, but the gift of God is eternal life through Jesus Christ our Lord."* (Romans 6:23)

To sum up the concept in a simple and understandable way, salvation is forgiveness. Forgiveness is necessary because each and every human is a sinful and unworthy creature. Remember, God is perfect, and as a result, He hates sin.

2.) The second step towards salvation is to believe the Word of God and to believe in the sinless perfection of Jesus Christ.

As I explained earlier, each person is a sinner, and we must be forgiven for that sin in order to have fellowship with God. This is evidenced in God's word, in Romans:

*"For all have sinned, and come short of the glory of God."* (Romans 3:23)

Even though we are not worthy of that forgiveness, God loves us enough to give us a way out of our miserable nature of sinfulness. God's provision was the birth of His Son, Jesus Christ.

*"For God so loved the world that he gave his only begotten Son, that whosoever believeth in him should not perish, but have everlasting life."* (John 3:16)

Remember, Christ lived a perfect life, so he was able to represent that sacrifice of bloodshed that was required. Christ took the sin of each and every person and gave His life in payment for them.

*"But God commendeth his love toward us, in that, while we were yet sinners, Christ died for us."* (Romans 5:8)

He was crucified (nailed to a cross by his hands and feet, enduring indescribable pain, and finally suffocating), which was a horrifying way to die. He was innocent, yet He still did this for each of us. He could have chosen not to follow through with the painful task of dying on that cross. He pleaded with God, that there might be another way.

*"36 ...Abba, Father, all things are possible unto thee; take away this cup from me: nevertheless not what I will, but what thou wilt."* (Mark 14:36)

Even so, it had to be done. He did it, and He did it for each and every one of us!

Even though Christ died, He did not remain in his tomb afterward. Instead, He conquered death, and was resurrected. The stone was rolled away from the front of His tomb, and He was not there! There were many witnesses who watched Jesus die, and then saw that He was alive again, three days later!

*"4 And when they looked, they saw that the stone was rolled away: for it was very great, 6...Be not affrighted: Ye seek Jesus of Nazareth, which was crucified: he is risen; he is not here: behold the place where they laid him 9 Now when Jesus was risen early the first day of the week, he appeared first to Mary Magdalene..."* (Mark 16:4, 6, 9)

He is alive today, in Heaven, preparing a place for those who believe in Him and who accept His gift of forgiveness and salvation. Jesus will come back again some day, and take each believer into an eternal life of fellowship with Him.

*"2 In my Father's house are many mansions: if it were not so, I would have told you. I go to prepare a place for you. 3 And if I go and prepare a place for you, I will come again, and receive you unto myself; that where I am, there ye may be also."* (John 13:2-3)

3.) The third step towards salvation is to understand the need to confess your sins.

There could never be enough appreciation in the world for us to express to Jesus, in light of all of the suffering He endured for us. However, one thing we can do that would be most pleasing to Him is to accept the gift that He made available to us by His suffering. Nothing hurts Him more than for someone to refuse His gift. In order to receive the gift of forgiveness and the salvation that comes with it, all we have to do is believe in Him, and ask for forgiveness! It is amazing how easy it can be, but it will transform your heart and your life for all of eternity.

*"If we confess our sins, he is faithful and just to forgive us our sins, and to cleanse us from all unrighteousness."* (1 John 1:9)

*"...if thou shalt confess with thy mouth the Lord Jesus, and shalt believe in thine heart that God hath raised him from the dead, thou shalt be saved."* (Romans 10:9)

*"For whosoever shall call upon the name of the Lord shall be saved."* (Romans 10:13)

*"These things have I written unto you that believe on the name of the Son of God; that ye may know that ye have eternal life..."* (1 John 5:13a)

When people accept salvation, it is routinely said that they "have asked Jesus into their hearts." This can be somewhat confusing. God is three persons in One: the Father, the Son and the Holy Spirit. His ability to be three distinct persons, yet still to be only one God, is sometimes hard to understand. As believers, we are able to feel the presence of Jesus and God through the Holy Spirit. This is how we are able to enjoy that never-ending fellowship. The Holy Spirit is the Comforter that is mentioned in the following scriptures:

*"But the Comforter, which is the Holy Ghost, whom the Father will send in my name, he shall teach you all things, and bring all things to your remembrance, whatsoever I have said unto you."* (John 14:26)

*"But when the Comforter is come, whom I will send unto you from the Father, even the Spirit of truth, which proceedeth from the Father, he shall testify of me:"* (John 15:26)

*"Nevertheless I tell you the truth; It is expedient for you that I go away: for if I go not away, the Comforter will not come unto you; but if I depart, I will send him unto you."* (John 16:7)

These scriptures depict the time after Christ's resurrection. He appeared to his disciples and spent some time with them before he ascended into heaven. During this time, He explained to them that when He ascended to heaven, He would send the Comforter, or the Holy Spirit, to each of them. Each one of us who accepts Christ will receive that Comforter when we ask for forgiveness and receive salvation. The presence of the comforting Holy Spirit in our hearts helps to guide us and protect us throughout our lives. This is another way we are able to enjoy never-ending fellowship with God.

4.) The last step towards salvation is to pray and ask forgiveness.

Here is a guiding prayer that you can say in order to accept the gift of forgiveness and salvation:

*Dear Lord - I believe that the Bible is truly Your word. I believe that Jesus Christ was the only perfect human who ever lived. Because He was perfect, I know that He was the only one who could serve as the sacrifice for my sins. I believe that Jesus was crucified for my sins and He suffered and died on a cross. I believe that He arose from the tomb, and is alive today in Heaven, because His almighty power conquered death. I know I am a sinner, and I understand that I sin every day. I ask that You please forgive me of my sins, and help me to turn from them. I want to receive the gift of salvation that Jesus' suffering made available for me. Please send the Holy Spirit into my heart to comfort and guide me. Please accept me as your forgiven child, and allow me to experience eternal fellowship with You; I pray these things in Jesus' name, Amen.*

If you prayed this prayer for the first time, you are a new creation through the gift of forgiveness and love through Christ. Congratulations! I cannot wait to see you someday in heaven!

5.) Now that you are saved, you should know you will not lose your salvation.

Even though each one of us will sin countless times every day, even after salvation, the Holy Spirit speaks to us, and guides us away from such behavior. Over time, we should sin less and less. Even so, we will still be tempted, and we will fail. As humans, it is in our nature. Thankfully, when we asked for that gift of salvation, it was granted. It will never be taken away from us. Often people refer to salvation as being "born again." That is a great way to envision our status as God's child. Once you are born, you cannot become "unborn." In the same manner of thinking, once you are a child of God, you will always be a child of God.

While we should pray and ask forgiveness for our sins on a regular basis, our certainty regarding our salvation should be solid. Once you are truly saved, you will always be saved. The scriptures offer us this comforting reassurance:

*"For I am persuaded, that neither death, nor life, nor angels, nor principalities, nor powers, nor things present, nor things to come, Nor height, nor depth, nor any other creature, shall be able to separate us from the love of*

*God, which is in Christ Jesus our Lord."* (Romans 8:38-39)

*"...I will never leave thee, nor forsake thee."* (Hebrews 13:5b)

# Final Words

Over the years I have made several decisions and choices which I have grown to regret later (some are evidenced by the stories in this book). I think everyone does this, to some extent, during their lives. However, on several occasions in my life, and for reasons still unknown to me, I purposefully and perpetually chose to do things which I knew were completely contrary to everything I have ever been taught. Even so, God loved me enough to provide people along the way who would re-direct me and help me to see that my actions were damaging and non-productive.

The worst thing about those times in my life is that I absolutely annihilated my Christian witness for many of those around me. There will be those who read this book and remember times when aspects of my life such as attitude, purity, language, and overall thought life were not sound. During those occasions my reputation as a Christian was drastically compromised. For those who were in my life during that time, I would like to apologize for my irresponsibility and ignorance. I feel the need to ask forgiveness simply because I cringe at the notion that my behavior could damage the credibility of Christian faith, in general. That being said, we all sin and make mistakes on a regular basis. Thankfully, God has forgiven me for those mistakes. Even so, I pray that anyone who may have been affected by my shortcomings will forgive me, as well.

If even just one person should come to know Christ as a result of this book, it will be worth all the time and work it took to publish. I have recently become addicted to the feeling of knowing that I had a part in spreading the Word of God to someone who needed and wanted to hear it. It brings me great joy, and it is an addiction that I am trying to feed as often as possible. My biggest struggle, however, is the elimination of my stubborn human pride – that is, the notion that I had any part in the equation when someone becomes a believer. Through that struggle with my human condition I am learning that nothing is possible without God and the guiding hand of the Holy Spirit. I am simply a conduit through which He can do His work. As a result, I am simply and humbly honored to be used for His purposes. Because of this, I cannot contain that overwhelming joy when someone new accepts Christ and joins His eternal family.

I had the honor and joy of helping to lead a very close friend to the Lord this spring, and nothing compares to the feeling of knowing that I will be able to see my loved one throughout eternity because she has become a believer. On the other hand, I must admit that I hesitated to share the Gospel with her, for fear that she would not want to hear it, and that her rejection of the truth would strain our friendship. What a knucklehead I am! If you care about someone – how in the world can you not talk to them and be assured that he or she will come to the saving knowledge of Christ? How can you not let them know that you care about the eternal state of their soul? How can you not step out on faith, and help your friend or family member with *the most important decision she or he will ever make?* After all, these are the people we know, love, and those who know us best. If we cannot talk to them about such meaningful and important issues, what is our problem (not a rhetorical question)? Furthermore, how can we possibly help others who may need it when we cannot even communicate with our own loved ones?

I was wrestling with those same questions when, believe it or not, my friend *approached me* and *asked me* how to know Christ. I became deeply ashamed of myself. That is when I realized that we, as believers, must step out on our faith and do what we know is right, without hesitation. I am still challenged by this truth because, although it gets easier over time, it may never become second nature for many of us to approach someone and bring up the subject of salvation. There are people all around us who yearn to know the truth. As ambivalent as we are when it comes to the challenge of approaching them with a conversation about God, just imagine how hard it must be for them to muster up the courage to ask someone about these things! Don't take a chance on losing a friend or family member for eternity! Make sure that you take the initiative to spread the gospel to those around you. It is my prayer for God to give you strength, courage, peace, and blessings in all of your future endeavors for Him.